The AI Leadership Edge
via ChatGPT, Copilot & Gemini
with 111 Prompts to Outperform

The AI Leadership Edge via ChatGPT, Copilot & Bard with 111 Prompts to Outperform

Achieve Competitive Advantage with AI-Powered Coaching, Mentoring & Leadership Skills for Business & Entrepreneurship

Mindscape Artwork Publishing
Mauricio Vasquez

Toronto, Canada

DEDICATION

To the industrious individuals and emerging executives committed to enhancing their leadership acumen: This book aims to be your trusted advisor, offering key insights to help you succeed in the multifaceted world of modern business.

INTRODUCTION

Welcome to the definitive book that synergizes traditional wisdom in mentoring, coaching, and leadership with the cutting-edge advancements of Generative Artificial Intelligence (AI). Written by Mauricio Vasquez, a recognized expert in both professional development and AI-enabled strategies, this book is designed to be a go-to resource for a broad spectrum of professionals seeking transformative impact in their careers and organizations.

In a world where the professional landscape is constantly evolving, accompanied by unrelenting demands for efficiency, innovation, and leadership, this book equips you with robust, data-informed strategies, all fine-tuned by the capabilities of Generative AI. Here, the focus transcends the realm of standard best practices, aiming to forge actionable, individualized pathways that result in concrete, measurable success.

Generative AI is not a mere trend but rather an invaluable co-pilot on your journey towards professional excellence. This book unpacks its wide-ranging utility, showcasing how AI can shape personalized mentorship frameworks, inform novel coaching strategies, and catalyze powerful leadership dynamics.

Our mission is explicit: to significantly augment your professional competencies, irrespective of your career stage or field. Whether you're an emerging talent, a seasoned executive, or someone on the lookout for disruptive innovations, this book is enriched with a blend of practical guidelines and state-of-the-art methodologies.

This book is more than an array of tools or techniques; it is an invitation to reshape your professional paradigm fundamentally. Be prepared to explore the art and science of compelling leadership, the optimization of AI-generated prompts, and the complex landscape of professional development.

Set sail on this journey to attain unparalleled professional acumen and influence. You are now on the threshold of a new period in professional excellence and human impact. Welcome to your next evolution.

ABOUT THE AUTHOR

Mauricio Vasquez is a multifaceted professional with over 20 years of experience in risk management and insurance, specializing in sectors like mining, power, and renewable energy. He holds an Industrial Engineering degree, a Master's in Business Administration, and a Master's in Marketing and Commercial Management, along with certifications in Enterprise Risk Management and Artificial Intelligence.

Mauricio is also a certified Adler Trained Coach and a self-published author, focusing on personal growth and professional development. His expertise in Artificial Intelligence and Large Language Models Prompt engineering adds a unique layer to his professional background. Fluent in both English and Spanish, Mauricio has worked across Canada, the U.S., Latin America, and the Caribbean. In addition to his corporate roles, he is a Professional and Life Coach, committed to helping immigrants transition successfully to new lives in Canada. His approach is deeply rooted in building long-term relationships and providing tailored, impactful solutions to clients.

If you want to connect with Mauricio, go to this link
https://www.linkedin.com/in/mauriciovasquez or scan this QR code:

WHAT IS GENERATIVE ARTIFICIAL INTELLIGENCE (AI)?

At the forefront of Artificial Intelligence (AI) advancements, Generative AI stands not merely as a milestone but as a significant saga that reshapes the contours of AI capabilities. It is important to clarify that this innovation does not represent an incremental refinement in data analytics. Rather, it's artificial intelligence capable of generating text, images, or other media, using generative models.

Traditional AI models excel in data analysis, focusing on pattern recognition and predictive analytics. Generative AI distinguishes itself by producing wholly original content infused with value. This covers a wide array of applications, from the composition of highly persuasive emails to the architecture of complex strategic initiatives, as well as the enhancement of dialogues in coaching and mentoring scenarios. In doing so, Generative AI serves to amplify human abilities, while fundamentally altering the landscape for innovative interactions with others.

This remarkable capability is rooted in intricate architectures of neural networks. Unlike simpler algorithms, Generative AI transcends mere mimicry of human patterns. It assimilates and extrapolates intricate human behavioral nuances, thereby extending its applicability to various sectors. The impact is nothing short of transformative, affecting realms as diverse as marketing strategy, executive leadership, and even personal development. This is not a theoretical exercise; it is an applied innovation with immediate, practical, and extensive implications for multiple industries.

As we transition to the forthcoming chapter focusing on Natural Language Processing (NLP) Chatbots, it is essential to acknowledge that Generative AI forms the architectural foundation for these advanced conversational interfaces. Within the specialized fields of coaching, mentoring, and leadership development, Generative AI enriches these platforms by enabling conversations that are not only relevant but also deeply contextual and emotionally resonant. The outcome is an enhanced coaching paradigm, enriched by insights that are simultaneously data-driven and imbued with human-like nuance. To overlook the capabilities of Generative AI is to relinquish untapped opportunities for innovation and heightened effectiveness.

WHAT ARE NATURAL LANGUAGE PROCESSING CHATBOTS?

An Artificial Intelligence (AI) Chatbot is a program within a website or app that uses machine learning (ML) and natural language processing (NLP) to interpret inputs and understand the intent behind a request or "prompt" (more on this later in the book). Chatbots can be rule-based with simple use cases or more advanced and able to handle multiple conversations.

The rise of language models like GPT has revolutionized the landscape of conversational AI. These Chatbots now boast advanced capabilities that can mimic not just a human conversation style but also a (super) human mind. They can find information online and produce unique content and insights.

The most important thing to know about an AI Chatbot is that it combines ML and NLP to understand what people need and bring the best answers. Some AI Chatbots are better for personal use, like conducting research, and others are best for business use, like featuring a Chatbot on your company's website.

With this in mind, we've compiled a list of the best AI Chatbots at the time of the writing of this book. We strongly suggest that you try and test each of the most popular ones and see what works best for you.

ChatGPT:
- Uses NLP to understand the context of conversations to provide related and original responses in a human-like conversation.
- Multiple use cases for things like answering questions, ideating and getting inspiration, or generating new content [like a marketing email].
- Improves over time as it has more conversations.

Microsoft Copilot/Bing Chat:
- Uses NLP and ML to understand conversation prompts.
- The compose feature can generate original written content and images, and its powerful search engine capabilities can surface answers from the web.
- It's a conversational tool, so you can continue sending messages until you're satisfied.

Google Gemini/Bard:
- Google's Bard is a multi-use AI Chatbot.
- It's powered by Google's LaMDA [instead of GPT].
- Use it for things like brainstorming and ideation, drafting unique and original content, or getting answers to your questions.
- Connected to Google's website index so it can access information from the internet.

Meta LLaMa:
- Meta's Chatbot is an open source large language [LLM].
- The tool is trained using reinforcement learning from human feedback [RLHF], learning from the preferences and ratings of human AI trainers.

Starting from now, we will refer to these platforms as Chatbots. For a guide on how to sign up to each, please refer to Appendix No 1.

If you're seeking a beginner-friendly, step-by-step guide to using ChatGPT, please refer to Appendix No. 3. This appendix includes access to our report, "Elevate Your Productivity Using ChatGPT," which offers a detailed guide on leveraging ChatGPT to boost efficiency and productivity across a range of professional environments.

As of the book's publication date, the information herein is current and accurate. The Chatbot industry, however, is dynamic, with constant updates and new entrants. While specifics may evolve, our prompts, core strategies and principles discussed in this book are designed to withstand the test of time, offering you a robust framework for navigating this fast-paced landscape.

THE BENEFITS OF USING AI CHATBOTS IN YOUR COACHING, MENTORING AND LEADERSHIP JOURNEY

In today's rapidly evolving corporate landscape, the pursuit of effective leadership, coaching, and mentorship resembles a full-time commitment. Traditional approaches often require significant time and resources, but the advent of Chatbots and advanced conversational platforms like ChatGPT is a game-changer.

These AI-driven tools are becoming invaluable assets in the realm of professional development. They offer real-time coaching, behavioral insights, and actionable strategies, which can be a boon for anyone aiming to climb the corporate ladder or make an impact as a leader.

The advantages of integrating Chatbots and the insights from this book into your leadership journey can be broken down into five key areas:

1. **Efficiency:** Chatbots can offer rapid, on-the-fly guidance that can dramatically expedite your leadership development cycle. They can help you formulate strategies, prepare for complex conversations, or even fine-tune your leadership philosophy.
2. **Quality:** While the advice or strategies generated by Chatbots won't be perfect, they provide a solid starting point. By issuing clear and specific prompts, you can glean actionable advice that can be fine-tuned to meet your unique leadership challenges.
3. **Edge:** In leadership, the ability to personalize your approach can be a unique advantage. Chatbots enable this level of personalization at scale. This allows you to adapt your leadership style and strategies to suit the distinct characteristics and needs of your team or organization, thereby standing out as a responsive leader.
4. **Innovative Insights:** Beyond standard guidance, Chatbots can be a springboard for creative thought. With the right queries, you can unlock best practices and innovative leadership strategies that you can apply to your unique context.
5. **Enhanced Self-Awareness:** This book is designed to be a robust tool to empower you in leadership and coaching roles. Coupled with Chatbots, you gain a more personalized form of guidance that can validate your skills and ambitions, boosting your confidence and equipping you to face a variety of leadership challenges.

By skillfully combining Chatbots with the actionable insights and strategies provided through this book, you're setting the stage for a potent blend of traditional wisdom and state-of-the-art technology. This fusion is set to redefine the frameworks of leadership, coaching, and mentorship in today's complex business environment.

WHAT ARE PROMPTS?

Imagine stepping into a high-stakes negotiation with only half the information—you're likely to miss the mark. Similarly, Chatbots rely on well-crafted prompts to deliver precise and valuable responses.

Prompts serve as the guiding questions, suggestions, or ideas that instruct Chatbots on how and what to respond. But these aren't just any text or phrase; prompts are carefully engineered inputs designed to optimize the Chatbot's output for quality, relevance, and accuracy.

Prompts are suggestions, questions, or ideas for what Chatbots should respond. And for Chatbots to provide a helpful response to their users, they need a thorough prompt with some background information and relevant context. Becoming a solid prompt writer takes time and experience, but there are also some best practices that you can use to see success fairly quickly:

1. **Be precise in your instructions:** when interacting with Chatbots for leadership or coaching tasks, specificity is paramount. Clearly define the tone, scope, and objectives you wish the Chatbot to achieve. For instance, you might say, "Generate a team motivational message that emphasizes the importance of collaboration and aligns with our Q4 targets. Keep the message under 150 words and use a motivational tone."
2. **Integrate contextual information:** the more context you provide, the better Chatbots can tailor their responses. Always include any relevant background information or guidelines. For example, in the case of crafting a message to resolve team conflicts, you may want to append specific issues or arguments that the team is facing.
3. **Segment your interactions:** complex leadership tasks often have multiple components. Break these down into discrete tasks and use individual prompts for each. If you're generating materials for a leadership workshop, you could use separate prompts for the introduction, body, and conclusion segments.
4. **Continuous refinement:** Chatbots provide a valuable starting point but shouldn't replace your own expertise and voice. Use the generated material as a draft that can be further honed and personalized. This ensures that the content aligns with your unique leadership style and the specific needs of your team or mentees.
5. **Employ follow-up prompts:** to get more nuanced advice, use follow-up prompts based on initial outputs. For example, if your first prompt is, "Outline the key principles for effective leadership," a good follow-up could be, "Explain the application of each principle in remote team settings." This sequencing enriches the dialogue and makes the Chatbot's advice more actionable. Check Appendix No 2 for 1100 follow-up prompts you could use, but remember they also need to be tailored to the specific conversation you are having with the Chatbot.

HOW TO USE THIS BOOK?

In the current professional ecosystem, the topics of coaching, mentoring, and leadership are intricate but filled with unprecedented opportunities. This book offers a comprehensive guide for leveraging artificial intelligence, specifically Chatbots, to gain a competitive edge in these sectors. While the content is structured around key frameworks and principles of leadership and coaching, you are encouraged to engage with this book in a non-linear fashion, focusing on areas most relevant to your immediate and long-term objectives.

1. **Optimize your outcomes with our specialized GPT:** We are thrilled to provide exclusive access to "*My Coaching, Mentoring & Leadership Advisor*" GPT, a cutting-edge tool developed using OpenAI's ChatGPT technology. This custom GPT model is specifically designed to offer targeted assistance in leadership, coaching, and mentoring, enhancing your professional journey with AI-driven insights. To maximize its impact, we recommend using this GPT in conjunction with the prompts provided in this book. This synergistic approach will amplify your learning experience, offering a unique blend of expert guidance and personalized AI assistance. To access this GPT, please refer to the following chapter in this book.

2. **Prompt engineering for optimal outcomes:** We advocate for an informed, strategic approach to using the prompts provided in this book. Each prompt is meticulously engineered to serve a specific purpose and is accompanied by its intended goal, a guiding formula, and two illustrative examples. Text highlighted in **bold** and terms enclosed in square brackets **[ ]** are particularly conducive to customization. We encourage you to not just copy these prompts verbatim but to understand their underlying structure and adapt them to your unique circumstances. The more tailored the prompt, the more relevant and actionable the output will be.

3. **Differentiating complexities for broader utility:** The aim is to offer a broader perspective on how these prompts can be employed and customized. By engaging with a diverse array of prompts, you can develop a nuanced understanding of their underlying mechanisms, thereby gaining the flexibility to tailor them to multiple contexts or objectives.

4. **Integrative strategies for customization:** As you move through this book, you are encouraged to blend different strategies and tools to create customized plans. A well-crafted prompt elicits a higher-quality response; thus, investment in tailoring your inquiries is more than just a recommendation—it's a necessity for meaningful engagement with the book's content.

5. **Ethical considerations and critical thinking:** AI provides valuable insights, but it's crucial to critically evaluate this information. Use Chatbots' advice as a starting point for your strategies, complementing it with further research and ethical considerations. It's essential to remember that while AI can augment decision-making, it can't replace human wisdom.

6. **Communication excellence:** When crafting prompts for Chatbots, aim for clarity and precision. Open-ended questions often lead to more in-depth responses. For a tailored experience, you can also specify the persona or role you want the AI to assume, thereby aligning its feedback with your specific leadership or coaching context.

7. **Target audience, industry, and specificity:** Clearly defining your target audience and industry will enable you to fine-tune the strategies and insights you derive from this book and the accompanying AI resources. Whether you are a leadership consultant, executive coach, or HR professional, audience specificity enhances the utility of the guidance offered.

8. **Getting started with Chatbots:** For those new to the Chatbots platform, we provide a step-by-step guide to get you up and running, empowering you to leverage AI capabilities for your professional development in leadership and coaching.

Here is an overview of the appendices and how they can be integrated into your prompting:

- **Appendix No. 4** - Professions in Mentoring, Coaching, and Leadership: This appendix enumerates key professions that support personal and organizational development through guidance, training, and inspiration. Select the profession most relevant to your current challenge or opportunity to tailor your prompts, ensuring the most pertinent input from the Chatbot.

- **Appendix No. 5** - Specializations in Mentoring, Coaching, and Leadership: This section presents specialized roles within these fields, emphasizing excellence, innovation, and resilience in professional settings. Choose a specialization closely aligned with your specific challenge or opportunity to create effective prompts and receive the most relevant input from the Chatbot.
- **Appendix No. 6** - Tones for Responses from Chatbots: This appendix explores various writing tones you may want Chatbots to use in their responses to your prompts, ensuring alignment with your communication preferences.
- **Appendix No. 7** - Writing Styles for Responses from Chatbots: This section explores a variety of writing styles designed to enhance the clarity and effectiveness of the responses you seek to obtain from Chatbots, ensuring tailored and impactful communication.
- **Appendix No. 8** - Tagging System for Prompt Navigation: This appendix extends beyond the table of contents by offering three tags for each prompt in the book. These tags are carefully selected to assist readers in easily finding the most relevant prompts for their specific challenges or opportunities, ensuring a targeted and efficient use of the book's resources.

By strategically integrating AI tools and best practices, you can enhance not just your personal growth, but also the development of those you coach, mentor, and lead.

MEET "*MY COACHING, MENTORING & LEADERSHIP ADVISOR*" GPT

My Coaching, Mentoring & Leadership Advisor GPT, developed with OpenAI's ChatGPT technology, enhances your interaction with ChatGPT, offering a more tailored and responsive experience.

This custom GPT (Generative Pre-trained Transformer) model is expertly crafted to provide targeted help in leadership, coaching, and mentoring.

As a dynamic Artificial Intelligence companion, it aligns with your unique professional style and needs, providing tailored advice and insights to help navigate your leadership path.

Engaging with this GPT is incredibly intuitive, and simpler than you might expect. Once you access to ChatGPT, you'll be greeted by a user-friendly interface where you can input your questions or prompts.

The GPT responds almost instantly, offering valuable insights and guidance.

Whether you aim to enhance your leadership abilities, improve team dynamics, or foster personal and professional growth, *My Coaching, Mentoring & Leadership Advisor GPT* stands as your gateway to innovative professional development.

Accompanying this section there two screenshots showcasing the user interface you'll encounter when accessing 'My Coaching, Mentoring & Leadership Advisor' GPT. This visual reference provides a clear preview of what to expect, guiding you through your first steps in utilizing this innovative tool.

To start your journey towards advanced leadership and coaching skills, and to experience this unique blend of knowledge and technology, please scan this QR code.

Disclaimer: There's a monthly fee for using OpenAI's Plus plan, which you need to access the GPT I created for this book. Wanted to be clear – I don't get any income from OpenAI for suggesting their service. It's all about giving you great tools, and that's why I produced this GPT specifically for the book and for you. As of now, us GPT builders don't get a share of OpenAI's earnings, but if that ever changes – I'll update the disclaimer right away. Mauricio

FREE GOODWILL

Would you consider investing a minute to leave a lasting impression on someone's professional journey? Your experience and insights matter.

Right now, there's a professional, a mentor, or a leader seeking to elevate their capabilities. They're navigating the challenges of leadership, coaching, and perhaps even career transition. Your review could be a pivotal guide for them.

Think of reviews as more than just responses—they're endorsements, collective knowledge, and indicators of reliability. If this book offers you actionable insights or innovative strategies, could you share those experiences through a quick review? By doing so, you contribute to:

- Directing someone to tools and strategies that can heighten their leadership skills.
- Facilitating an individual's capacity to better mentor and coach.
- Enriching someone's perspective, which they might have otherwise overlooked.
- Catalyzing transformation in another's professional path.

By reviewing this book, you contribute to broadening the horizon of effective leadership, mentorship, and coaching for someone else. If you find value in this book, don't hesitate to share it within your network. People remember fondly those who introduced them to beneficial resources.

Your engagement is much appreciated. Thank you for becoming an advocate for impactful leadership and personal development.

Best regards,

Mauricio

P.S. To leave your review, please scan this QR code:

Scan the QR code to access our book collection.

TABLE OF CONTENTS

ACCOUNTABILITY

PROMPT No 1

Tags

Accountability - Manager Review - Professionalism

Goal

To equip professionals with a structured, respectful, and assertive approach for holding their manager accountable during a performance review, thereby enhancing the quality of leadership and fostering a culture of mutual accountability.

Prompt

As a **Professional Coach** specializing in **career development** within the **insurance industry**, provide an exhaustive and meticulous examination, incorporating innovative insights and inventive strategies, for outlining a nuanced approach that individuals can employ during a performance review to respectfully and assertively hold their manager accountable for various aspects such as **setting clear expectations, providing timely feedback, and ensuring a supportive work environment**. Additionally, offer insights into how to prepare for potential pushbacks and secure mutual understanding and respect.

Formula

As a **[profession]** specializing in **[topic/field]** within the **[industry]**, provide an exhaustive and meticulous examination, incorporating innovative insights and inventive strategies, for outlining a nuanced approach that individuals can employ during a [performance review] to respectfully and assertively hold their manager accountable for various aspects such as **[setting clear expectations/providing timely feedback/ensuring a supportive work environment]**. Additionally, offer insights into how to prepare for potential pushbacks and secure mutual understanding and respect.

Examples

Example 1: As a Career Advisor specializing in employee relations within the tech industry, provide an exhaustive and meticulous examination, incorporating innovative insights and inventive strategies, for outlining a nuanced approach that engineers can employ during a performance review to respectfully and assertively hold their manager accountable for aspects like technical mentorship, agile project management, and team collaboration. Additionally, offer insights into how to prepare for potential pushbacks and secure mutual understanding and respect.

Example 2: As an HR Consultant specializing in leadership accountability within the healthcare sector, provide an exhaustive and meticulous examination, incorporating innovative insights and inventive strategies, for outlining a nuanced approach that nurses and clinicians can employ during a performance review to respectfully and assertively hold their manager accountable for areas like patient care oversight, staff scheduling, and professional development. Additionally, offer insights into how to prepare for potential pushbacks and secure mutual understanding and respect.

PROMPT No 2

Tags

Effort Acknowledgment - Team Commitment - Appreciative Strategy

Goal

To gain insights on specific strategies or actions that can be employed to effectively acknowledge and value the diligent efforts and unwavering commitment exhibited by each member of a team.

As a **Leadership Coach**, adopting an **appreciative and respectful tone**, could you provide specific strategies or actions that I can employ to ensure that I effectively acknowledge and value the **diligent efforts and unwavering commitment** exhibited by each member of **my team**?

As a **[profession]**, adopting a **[tone of voice]**, could you provide specific strategies or actions that **[I/Name/Role]** can employ to ensure that **[I/Name/Role]** effectively acknowledges and values the **[contextual challenge/opportunity]** exhibited by each member of **[my/their] [team/group/department]**?

Example 1: As a Human Resources Consultant, adopting a supportive and appreciative tone, could you provide specific strategies or actions that a department head can employ to ensure that they effectively acknowledge and value the diligent efforts and unwavering commitment exhibited by each member of their logistic team?

Example 2: As a Team Coach, adopting a positive and respectful tone, could you provide specific strategies or actions that I can employ to ensure that I effectively acknowledge and value the diligent efforts and unwavering commitment exhibited by each member of my investment management team?

ACTION

PROMPT No 3

Business Planning - Detailed Explanation - Organizational Structure

To meticulously outline and comprehend the multifaceted process of crafting a robust business plan, ensuring a clear trajectory towards business objectives and a concrete foundation for operational, financial, and strategic decision-making.

As a **Business Consultant**, with a focus on **clarity and precision**, could you delineate a step-by-step methodology to **devise a comprehensive and well-structured business plan**? This discussion should meticulously cover **each phase of the process**, the significance of each **step**, and how they collectively contribute to **a sound business blueprint** capable of **guiding organizational decision-making and tracking progress towards defined objectives**.

As a **[Profession]**, with a focus on **[desired tone attributes]**, could you delineate a step-by-step methodology to **[specific task or objective]**? This discussion should meticulously cover **[key areas or steps]**, the significance of each **[step/phase/element]**, and how they collectively contribute to **[desired outcome or final product]** capable of **[further benefits or implications]**.

Example 1: As a Financial Advisor, with a focus on analytical rigor and precision, could you delineate a step-by-step methodology to create a comprehensive and well-organized financial plan? This discussion should meticulously cover each phase of the planning process, the significance of each step, and how they collectively contribute to a sound financial framework capable of guiding investment decisions and safeguarding financial security.

Example 2: As a Marketing Strategist, with a focus on creativity and coherence, could you delineate a step-by-step methodology to develop a comprehensive and well-structured marketing plan? This discussion should meticulously cover each phase of the strategizing process, the significance of each step, and how they collectively contribute to a potent marketing blueprint capable of driving brand recognition and market share growth.

PROMPT No 4

Tags

Team Dynamics - Goal Accomplishment - Behavioral Mitigation

Goal

To gain a comprehensive analysis of methods and strategies that a team can utilize to identify and mitigate activities or behaviors that impede progress or negatively impact team dynamics, and to learn about effective measures for enhancing team dynamics and achieving goals.

Prompt

As a **Team Development Consultant**, adopting a **solution-oriented and analytical tone**, could you provide a comprehensive analysis outlining the various methods and strategies that **my team** can utilize to accurately identify and mitigate any activities or behaviors that impede their progress in **meeting their quota or have a detrimental effect on team dynamics**? Moreover, could you suggest measures that have proven to be effective in **enhancing team dynamics and bringing the team closer to accomplishing their goals**?

Formula

As a **[profession]**, adopting a **[tone of voice]**, could you provide a comprehensive analysis outlining the various methods and strategies that **[my/their]** **[team/group/department]** can utilize to accurately identify and mitigate any activities or behaviors that impede their progress in **[contextual challenge/opportunity]**? Moreover, could you suggest measures that have proven to be effective in **[desired outcome]**?

Examples

Example 1: As a Leadership Development Consultant, adopting a constructive and analytical tone, could you provide a comprehensive analysis outlining the various methods and strategies that a sales team can utilize to accurately identify and mitigate any activities or behaviors that impede their progress in meeting their sales targets or have a detrimental effect on team dynamics? Moreover, could you suggest measures that have proven to be effective in enhancing team dynamics and bringing the sales team closer to accomplishing their goals?

Example 2: As a Team Coach, adopting a solution-oriented and analytical tone, could you provide a comprehensive analysis outlining the various methods and strategies that my project team can utilize to accurately identify and mitigate any activities or behaviors that impede their progress in meeting their project deadlines or have a detrimental effect on team dynamics? Moreover, could you suggest measures that have proven to be effective in enhancing team dynamics and bringing the project team closer to accomplishing their goals?

Tags

Motivational Strategies - Perspective Expansion - Opportunity Pursuit

Goal

To gain a clear and detailed explanation of the specific strategies, techniques, and approaches that can be utilized to successfully motivate and encourage team members to expand their perspectives and actively pursue new opportunities for action.

Prompt

As a **Leadership Development Consultant**, adopting an **inspiring and motivational tone**, could you provide a clear and detailed explanation of the specific strategies, techniques, and approaches that can be utilized to successfully **motivate and encourage my team members to expand their perspectives and actively pursue new opportunities for action**?

Formula

As a **[profession]**, adopting a **[tone of voice]**, could you provide a clear and detailed explanation of the specific strategies, techniques, and approaches that can be utilized to successfully **[desired outcome]**?

Examples

Example 1: As a Team Coach, adopting a supportive and encouraging tone, could you provide a clear and detailed explanation of the specific strategies, techniques, and approaches that can be utilized to successfully motivate and encourage the sales team to expand their perspectives and actively pursue new opportunities for action?

Example 2: As a Management Consultant, adopting a clear and concise tone, could you provide a detailed explanation of the specific strategies, techniques, and approaches that can be utilized to successfully motivate and encourage the marketing team to expand their perspectives and actively pursue new opportunities for action?

AWARENESS

PROMPT No 6

Tags

Professional Growth - Development Evaluation - HR Strategies

Goal

To gain insights on the most effective methods and strategies to evaluate the current status of a team's professional growth and development.

Prompt

As a **Human Resources Consultant**, adopting an **analytical and insightful tone**, could you provide insights on the most effective methods and strategies to evaluate the current status of **my team's professional growth and development**? This is particularly relevant given the goal of **understanding and enhancing the professional development of the team**.

Formula

As a **[profession]**, adopting a **[tone of voice]**, could you provide insights on the most effective methods and strategies to evaluate the current status of **[my/their] [team/group/department]'s [contextual challenge/opportunity]**? This is particularly relevant given the goal of **[desired outcome]**.

Example 1: As a Leadership Development Consultant, adopting a thoughtful and analytical tone, could you provide insights on the most effective methods and strategies to evaluate the current status of the mergers and acquisitions team's professional growth and development? This is particularly relevant given the goal of understanding and enhancing the professional development of this team.

Example 2: As a Team Coach, adopting an insightful and constructive tone, could you provide insights on the most effective methods and strategies to evaluate the current status of my project team's professional growth and development? This is particularly relevant given the goal of understanding and enhancing the professional development of the project team.

PROMPT No 7

Self-Awareness - Performance - Management

To gain specific steps to assist a team in gaining a thorough understanding by themselves about the current state of their performance levels, fostering self-awareness and performance management.

Given the challenge of **understanding current performance levels**, as a **Performance Management Specialist** and in a **clear and concise tone**, could you suggest specific steps I can take to assist **my team** in **gaining a thorough understanding by themselves**?

Given the challenge of **[contextual challenge/opportunity]**, as a **[profession]** and in a **[tone of voice]**, could you suggest specific steps **[I/Name/Role]** can take to assist **[my/their] [team/group/department]** in **[desired outcome]**?

Example 1: Given the challenge of understanding current performance levels in a high-stress environment, as a Leadership Development Consultant and in a supportive and solution-oriented tone, could you suggest specific steps a department head can take to assist their faculty in gaining a thorough understanding by themselves?

Example 2: As a Human Resources Manager, in an encouraging and professional tone, could you suggest specific steps I can take to assist my sales team in gaining a thorough understanding by themselves about the current state of their performance levels? This advice is particularly relevant given the challenge of maintaining high performance in a competitive market.

PROMPT No 8

Identity Recognition - True Self - Personal Growth

To gain specific strategies or actions to effectively assist a team in recognizing and understanding the areas where their true personalities and desired identities coincide, fostering an enhancement in self-awareness and personal growth within the team.

As an **Executive Mentor**, adopting an **empathetic and respectful tone**, could you suggest specific strategies or actions that I can take to effectively assist **my team** in recognizing and understanding **the areas where their true personalities and desired identities coincide**? This is particularly relevant given the goal of enhancing self-awareness and personal growth within the team.

Formula

As a **[profession]**, adopting a **[tone of voice]**, could you suggest specific strategies or actions that **[I/Name/Role]** can take to effectively assist **[my/their]** **[team/group/department]** in recognizing and understanding **[contextual challenge/opportunity]**? This is particularly relevant given the goal of **[desired outcome]**.

Examples

Example 1: Adopting a supportive and considerate tone, as a Career Coach, could you suggest specific strategies or actions that a department head can take to effectively assist their faculty in recognizing and understanding the areas where their true personalities and desired identities coincide? This is particularly relevant given the goal of enhancing self-awareness and personal growth within the faculty.

Example 2: As a Leadership Development Consultant, adopting a patient and understanding tone, could you suggest specific strategies or actions that I can take to effectively assist my project team in recognizing and understanding the areas where their true personalities and desired identities coincide? This is particularly relevant given the goal of enhancing self-awareness and personal growth within the project team.

PROMPT No 9

Tags

Empowerment - Strategy - Contribution

Goal

To gain insights on how to leverage personal skills, expertise, and resources to make a meaningful and substantial contribution to the success and expansion of a company or team.

Prompt

As a **Business Coach**, adopting an **empowering and strategic tone**, could you provide specific actions that I can take to make a meaningful and substantial contribution to the success and expansion of **my company or team**, leveraging **my skills, expertise, and resources** in a way that adds **significant value and has a lasting impact**?

Formula

As a **[profession]**, adopting a **[tone of voice]**, could you provide specific actions that **[I/Name/Role]** can take to make a meaningful and substantial contribution to the success and expansion of **[my/their]** **[company/team/group]**, leveraging **[my/their]** **[contextual challenge/opportunity]** in a way that adds **[desired outcome]**?

Examples

Example 1: As a Leadership Consultant, adopting an inspiring and strategic tone, could you provide specific actions that a department head can take to make a meaningful and substantial contribution to the success and expansion of their department, leveraging their skills, expertise, and resources in a way that adds significant value and has a lasting impact?

Example 2: As a Career Coach, adopting a motivational and strategic tone, could you provide specific actions that I can take to make a meaningful and substantial contribution to the success and expansion of my startup, leveraging my skills, expertise, and resources in a way that adds significant value and has a lasting impact?

PROMPT No 10

Learning - Access - Productivity

To gain a thorough and detailed understanding of specific strategies or methods that can be used to successfully identify and access learning opportunities that directly contribute to enhancing the performance and productivity of a team.

As a **Learning and Development Specialist**, adopting an **informative and engaging tone**, could you provide a thorough and detailed response to the following question: What specific strategies or methods can I use to **successfully identify and access learning opportunities** that directly contribute to enhancing the performance and productivity of **my team**? This is particularly relevant given the goal of **fostering continuous learning and development within the team**.

As a **[profession]**, adopting a **[tone of voice]**, could you provide a thorough and detailed response to the following question: What specific strategies or methods can **[I/Name/Role]** use to **[contextual challenge/opportunity]** that directly contribute to enhancing the performance and productivity of **[my/their] [team/group/department]**? This is particularly relevant given the goal of **[desired outcome]**.

Example 1: As a Corporate Trainer, adopting an encouraging and supportive tone, could you provide a thorough and detailed response to the following question: What specific strategies or methods can a department head use to successfully identify and access learning opportunities that directly contribute to enhancing the performance and productivity of their faculty? This is particularly relevant given the goal of fostering continuous learning and development within the faculty.

Example 2: As a Talent Development Manager, adopting a clear and concise tone, could you provide a thorough and detailed response to the following question: What specific strategies or methods can I use to successfully identify and access learning opportunities that directly contribute to enhancing the performance and productivity of my project team? This is particularly relevant given the goal of fostering continuous learning and development within the project team.

PROMPT No 11

Assumptions - Strategies - Dynamics

To gain specific instructions on the strategies and techniques that can be employed to effectively uncover and expose the implicit assumptions that a team may have unknowingly depended on while carrying out their assignments or projects, fostering a deeper understanding of team dynamics and decision-making processes.

As a **Business Analyst**, adopting a **detailed and instructive tone**, could you provide specific instructions on the strategies and techniques I can employ to effectively uncover and expose the implicit assumptions that **my team** may have unknowingly depended on while carrying out their **assignments or projects**? This is particularly relevant given the goal of **fostering a deeper understanding of team dynamics and decision-making processes**.

As a **[profession]**, adopting a **[tone of voice]**, could you provide specific instructions on the strategies and techniques **[I/Name/Role]** can employ to **[contextual challenge/opportunity]** that **[my/their]** **[team/group/department]** may have unknowingly depended on while carrying out their **[assignments/tasks/projects]**? This is particularly relevant given the goal of **[desired outcome]**.

Example 1: As a Team Coach, adopting a clear and instructive tone, could you provide specific instructions on the strategies and techniques a project manager can employ to effectively uncover and expose the implicit assumptions that their project team may have unknowingly depended on while carrying out their tasks? This is particularly relevant given the goal of fostering a deeper understanding of team dynamics and decision-making processes within the project team.

Example 2: As an Organizational Psychologist, adopting a detailed and instructive tone, could you provide specific instructions on the strategies and techniques I can employ to effectively uncover and expose the implicit assumptions that my sales team may have unknowingly depended on while carrying out their sales pitches? This is particularly relevant given the goal of fostering a deeper understanding of team dynamics and decision-making processes within the sales team.

BELIEF

PROMPT No 12

Empowerment - Beliefs - Goals

To gain a detailed understanding of specific strategies that can be implemented to cultivate and proficiently convey positive beliefs, empowering a team to accomplish exceptionally ambitious goals or commitments.

As a **Leadership Development Consultant**, adopting an **inspiring and motivating tone**, could you provide a detailed explanation of specific strategies that I can implement to **cultivate and proficiently convey positive beliefs** within my team? This is particularly relevant given the goal of **empowering my team to accomplish exceptionally ambitious goals or commitments**.

As a **[profession]**, adopting a **[tone of voice]**, could you provide a detailed explanation of specific strategies that **[I/Name/Role]** can implement to **[contextual challenge/opportunity]** within **[my/their] [team/group/department]**? This is particularly relevant given the goal of **[desired outcome]**.

Examples

Example 1: Adopting an encouraging and supportive tone, as a Leadership Development Consultant, could you provide a detailed explanation of specific strategies that a department head can implement to cultivate and proficiently convey positive beliefs within their faculty? This is particularly relevant given the goal of empowering the faculty to accomplish exceptionally ambitious academic goals.

Example 2: As a Team Coach, adopting an enthusiastic and optimistic tone, could you provide a detailed explanation of specific strategies that I can implement to cultivate and proficiently convey positive beliefs within my project team? This is particularly relevant given the goal of empowering my project team to accomplish exceptionally ambitious project goals.

PROMPT No 13

Tags

Mindset - Performance - Belief

Goal

To gain insights on how to foster a specific belief or mindset within a team to address a particular problem that is causing a decrease in their performance.

Prompt

As a **Leadership Development Consultant**, adopting a **supportive and solution-oriented tone**, could you provide insights on how **I** can foster a specific belief or mindset **within my team** to address **the particular problem of lack of self-awareness**, which is leading to a decrease in their **performance**?

Formula

As a **[profession]**, adopting a **[tone of voice]**, could you provide insights on how **[I/Name/Role]** can foster a specific belief or mindset within **[my/their]** **[team/group/department]** to address **[contextual challenge/opportunity]**, which is leading to a decrease in their **[performance/productivity/effectiveness]**?

Examples

Example 1: As a Team Coach, adopting an encouraging and optimistic tone, could you provide insights on how I can foster a specific belief or mindset within my sales team to address the particular problem of lack of motivation, which is leading to a decrease in their sales performance?

Example 2: Adopting a supportive and solution-oriented tone, as a Management Consultant, could you provide insights on how a department head can foster a specific belief or mindset within their IT team to address the particular problem of lack of communication with other departments, which is leading to a decrease in their project effectiveness?

PROMPT No 14

Tags

Outcomes - Emotions - Evaluation

Goal

To gain a detailed understanding of the methods or strategies that a team can use to effectively assess the extent to which they find it beneficial to consider alternative outcomes, especially in terms of their emotional response to a problem.

As a **Team Development Consultant**, adopting a **supportive and insightful tone**, could you provide specific techniques or approaches that **my team** can employ to effectively assess the degree to which they perceive value in **exploring alternative solutions**, specifically in relation to their **emotional reaction to a problem**?

As a **[profession]**, adopting a **[tone of voice]**, could you provide specific techniques or approaches that **[my/their]** **[team/group/department]** can employ to effectively assess the degree to which they perceive value in **[contextual challenge/opportunity]**, specifically in relation to their **[desired outcome]**?

Example 1: As a Leadership Coach, adopting a compassionate and understanding tone, could you provide specific techniques or approaches that my marketing team can employ to effectively assess the degree to which they perceive value in exploring alternative marketing strategies, specifically in relation to their emotional reaction to the current campaign's performance?

Example 2: As an Organizational Psychologist, adopting a professional and empathetic tone, could you provide specific techniques or approaches that their sales team can employ to effectively assess the degree to which they perceive value in exploring alternative sales tactics, specifically in relation to their emotional reaction to the recent sales slump?

PROMPT No 15

Limitations - Independence - Progress

To provide a detailed guide on how a team can independently identify and address any assumptions or beliefs that might be limiting their progress or potential.

As a **Leadership Development Consultant**, adopting a **supportive and encouraging tone**, could you provide specific actions that **my team** can undertake on their own to thoroughly and effectively identify and uncover any **assumptions or beliefs** that might be hindering their advancement or limiting their potential?

As a **[profession]**, adopting a **[tone of voice]**, could you provide specific actions that **[my/their]** **[team/group/department]** can undertake on their own to thoroughly and effectively identify and uncover any **[contextual challenge/opportunity]** that might be hindering their advancement or limiting their potential?

Example 1: As a Team Coach, adopting a motivational and positive tone, could you provide specific actions that my sales team can undertake on their own to thoroughly and effectively identify and uncover any assumptions or beliefs that might be hindering their sales performance or limiting their potential?

Example 2: As a Business Consultant, adopting a professional and clear tone, could you provide specific actions that their marketing department can undertake on their own to thoroughly and effectively identify and uncover any assumptions or beliefs that might be hindering their campaign effectiveness or limiting their potential?

PROMPT No 16

Qualities - Development - Professionalism

To gain insights on how to guide a team towards understanding the professional qualities and skills they need to develop in order to excel in their roles.

As a **Leadership Development Consultant**, adopting a **supportive and encouraging tone**, could you provide specific strategies that I can employ to engage **my team** in meaningful discussions about the **professional qualities and skills they should develop in order to excel in their roles**?

As a **[profession]**, adopting a **[tone of voice]**, could you provide specific strategies that **[I/Name/Role]** can employ to engage **[my/their]** **[team/group/department]** in meaningful discussions about the **[contextual challenge/opportunity]**?

Example 1: As a Team Coach, adopting a motivational and empathetic tone, could you provide specific strategies that a department head can employ to engage their faculty in meaningful discussions about the academic qualities and skills they should develop in order to excel in their roles?

Example 2: As a Human Resources (HR) Consultant, adopting a clear and concise tone, could you provide specific strategies that I can employ to engage my operations management team in meaningful discussions about the leadership management qualities and skills they should develop in order to excel in their roles?

CHALLENGE

PROMPT No 17

Independence - Strategies - Motivation

To foster independent thinking within the team, enabling them to generate potential next steps for their tasks or projects on their own.

As a **Leadership Development Consultant**, adopting a **motivational and encouraging tone**, could you provide **strategies or techniques** that I can employ to **inspire and encourage my team members to independently generate potential next steps for the tasks or projects they are currently engaged in**?

As a **[profession]**, adopting a **[tone of voice]**, could you provide **[strategies/techniques/methods]** that **[I/Name/Role]** can employ to **[desired outcome]**?

Example 1: As a Management Consultant, adopting a motivational and encouraging tone, could you provide strategies that a department head can employ to inspire and encourage their IT team to independently generate potential next steps for their software development projects?

Example 2: As a Team Building Coach, adopting a supportive and inspiring tone, could you provide techniques that I can employ to inspire and encourage my marketing team to independently generate potential next steps for their ongoing marketing campaigns they are currently working on?

PROMPT No 18

Tags

Competencies - Emotional - Resolution

Goal

To understand the specific obstacles or issues that arise when a team lacks core competencies in dealing with a lack of emotional intelligence and to learn how to effectively resolve these challenges.

Prompt

As a **Leadership Trainer**, adopting a **supportive and solution-oriented tone**, could you provide specific obstacles or issues that arise when a team lacks core competencies in dealing with a lack of emotional intelligence? Additionally, could you provide strategies on how these challenges can be effectively resolved? This is particularly relevant given the goal of enhancing emotional intelligence within the team.

Formula

As a **[profession]**, adopting a **[tone]**, could you provide specific obstacles or issues that arise when **[my/their]** **[team/group/department]** lacks **[contextual challenge/opportunity]**? Additionally, could you provide strategies on how these challenges can be effectively resolved? This is particularly relevant given the goal of **[desired outcome]**.

Examples

Example 1: Adopting a supportive and solution-oriented tone, as a Leadership Trainer, could you provide specific obstacles or issues that arise when a sales team lacks core competencies in dealing with a lack of emotional intelligence? Additionally, could you provide strategies on how these challenges can be effectively resolved? This is particularly relevant given the goal of enhancing emotional intelligence within the sales team.

Example 2: As a Leadership Trainer, adopting a supportive and solution-oriented tone, could you provide specific obstacles or issues that arise when a marketing team lacks core competencies in dealing with a lack of emotional intelligence? Additionally, could you provide strategies on how these challenges can be effectively resolved? This is particularly relevant given the goal of enhancing emotional intelligence within the marketing team.

PROMPT No 19

Tags

Adaptability - Mindset - Leadership

To gain specific and detailed actions that can be implemented to effectively lead a team in embracing a new perspective or mindset, fostering adaptability and open-mindedness within the team.

Prompt

As a **Leadership Development Consultant**, adopting a **supportive and encouraging tone**, could you provide me with specific and detailed actions that **I** can implement to effectively lead **my team** in embracing a **new perspective or mindset**? This is particularly relevant given the goal of **fostering adaptability and open-mindedness within the team**.

Formula

As a **[profession]**, adopting a **[tone of voice]**, could you provide me with specific and detailed actions that **[I/Name/Role]** can implement to effectively lead **[my/their]** **[team/group/department]** in embracing a **[contextual challenge/opportunity]**? This is particularly relevant given the goal of **[desired outcome]**.

Examples

Example 1: As a Change Management Consultant, adopting a clear and concise tone, could you provide me with specific and detailed actions that I can implement to effectively lead my project team in embracing a new project management methodology? This is particularly relevant given the goal of fostering adaptability and open-mindedness within the project team.

Example 2: As a Team Coach, adopting a motivational and enthusiastic tone, could you provide me with specific and detailed actions that I can implement to effectively lead my sales team in embracing a new sales strategy? This is particularly relevant given the goal of fostering adaptability and open-mindedness within the sales team.

PROMPT No 20

Tags

Systematic - Organization - Guidance

Goal

To gain specific strategies or methods that can be implemented to effectively motivate and guide a team towards adopting a systematic and organized approach when faced with obstacles, with the aim of problem-solving and devising action plans.

Prompt

As a **Leadership Development Consultant**, adopting a **solution-oriented and professional tone**, could you recommend specific strategies or methods that **I** can implement to effectively motivate and guide **my team** towards adopting **a systematic and organized approach** when faced with **obstacles**, with the aim of **problem-solving and devising action plans**?

Formula

As a **[profession]**, adopting a **[tone of voice]**, could you recommend specific strategies or methods that **[I/Name/Role]** can implement to effectively motivate and guide **[my/their]** **[team/group/department]** towards adopting a **[desired outcome]** when faced with **[contextual challenge/opportunity]**, with the aim of **[desired outcome]**?

Examples

Example 1: As a Team Coach, adopting a supportive and encouraging tone, could you recommend specific strategies or methods that a project manager can implement to effectively motivate and guide their project team towards adopting a systematic and organized approach when faced with project-related obstacles, with the aim of problem-solving and devising action plans?

Example 2: As an Organizational Psychologist, adopting a clear and concise tone, could you recommend specific strategies or methods that I can implement to effectively motivate and guide my sales team towards adopting a systematic and organized approach when faced with sales-related obstacles, with the aim of problem-solving and devising action plans?

PROMPT No 21

Tags

Empowerment - Self-Discovery - Strategies

Goal

To gain specific strategies or methods that can be effectively utilized to accurately recognize and utilize personal strengths in order to triumph over obstacles or achieve success in a project.

Prompt

As a **Personal Development Coach**, adopting an **empowering and solution-oriented tone**, could you share specific strategies or methods that I can effectively utilize to accurately recognize and utilize **my** personal strengths in order to **triumph over obstacles or achieve success in my projects**?

Formula

As a **[profession]**, adopting a **[tone of voice]**, could you share specific strategies or methods that **[I/Name/Role]** can effectively utilize to accurately recognize and utilize **[my/their]** personal strengths in order to **[contextual challenge/opportunity]**?

Examples

Example 1: As a Career Coach, adopting a supportive and encouraging tone, could you share specific strategies or methods that a Chief Finance Officer can effectively utilize to accurately recognize and utilize their personal strengths in order to triumph over obstacles or achieve success in their refinancing negotiations?

Example 2: As a Leadership Consultant, adopting a motivational and professional tone, could you share specific strategies or methods that I can effectively utilize to accurately recognize and utilize my personal strengths in order to triumph over obstacles or achieve success in my team management?

PROMPT No 22

Tags

Risk-Taking - Team-Discussion - Positive-Outcome

Goal

To gain effective strategies for initiating a discussion with a team, encouraging them to share their experiences of taking risks that ultimately led to positive outcomes.

Prompt

As a **Leadership Consultant**, adopting an **engaging and supportive tone**, could you suggest effective strategies that I can employ to initiate a discussion with **my team**, encouraging them to share their experiences of **taking risks that ultimately led to positive outcomes**?

As a **[profession]**, adopting a **[tone of voice]**, could you suggest effective strategies that **[I/Name/Role]** can employ to initiate a discussion with **[my/their]** **[team/group/department]**, encouraging them to share their experiences of **[contextual challenge/opportunity]**?

Example 1: As a Team Development Coach, adopting an open and encouraging tone, could you suggest effective strategies that a department head can employ to initiate a discussion with their faculty, encouraging them to share their experiences of taking risks that ultimately led to breakthroughs in their research?

Example 2: As a Business Coach, adopting a respectful and engaging tone, could you suggest effective strategies that I can employ to initiate a discussion with my project team, encouraging them to share their experiences of taking risks that ultimately led to unsuccessful project outcomes?

CHANGE

PROMPT No 23

Sales-Communication - Obstacle-Resolution - Client-Service

To gain strategies or approaches for effectively communicating with a team about the specific areas in the sales process or client service process where they are facing the most challenges, and to understand the steps that can be taken to successfully address and overcome these obstacles.

As a **Sales Manager**, adopting a **solution-oriented and empathetic tone**, could you suggest strategies or approaches that **I** can employ to effectively communicate with **my team** about the specific areas in the **sales process or client service process** where we are facing the most challenges? Additionally, what steps can we take to successfully **address and overcome these obstacles**?

As a **[profession]**, adopting a **[tone of voice]**, could you suggest strategies or approaches that **[I/Name/Role]** can employ to effectively communicate with **[my/their]** **[team/group/department]** about the specific areas in the **[contextual challenge/opportunity]** where we are facing the most challenges? Additionally, what steps can we take to successfully **[desired outcome]**?

Example 1: As a Customer Service Manager, adopting a patient and understanding tone, could you suggest strategies or approaches that a team lead can employ to effectively communicate with their customer service team about the specific areas in the client service process where they are facing the most challenges? Additionally, what steps can they take to successfully address and overcome these obstacles?

Example 2: As a Business Coach, adopting a supportive and motivational tone, could you suggest strategies or approaches that I can employ to effectively communicate with my sales team about the specific areas in the sales process where we are facing the most challenges? Additionally, what steps can we take to successfully address and overcome these obstacles?

PROMPT No 24

Self-Motivation - Performance - Change

Goal

To gain strategies or methods that can be employed to motivate a team to independently contemplate the necessary changes they should make in order to enhance their performance.

Prompt

As a **Leadership Development Consultant**, adopting a **motivational and encouraging tone**, could you suggest strategies or methods that I can employ to motivate **my team** to independently contemplate the necessary changes they should make in order to enhance their performance?

Formula

As a **[profession]**, adopting a **[tone of voice]**, could you suggest strategies or methods that **[I/Name/Role]** can employ to motivate **[my/their]** **[team/group/department]** to independently contemplate the necessary changes they should make in order to **[desired outcome]**?

Examples

Example 1: As a Team Coach, adopting an inspiring and supportive tone, could you suggest strategies or methods that a HR department head can employ to motivate their recruitment team to independently contemplate the necessary changes they should make in order to enhance their performance?

Example 2: As a Performance Coach, adopting a positive and motivating tone, could you suggest strategies or methods that I can employ to motivate my project team to independently contemplate the necessary changes they should make in order to enhance their project execution?

PROMPT No 25

Transformation - Mindset - Improvement

Goal

To gain concrete and specific strategies and techniques to successfully shift a team's mindset and overall attitude, resulting in positive transformation and improvement, fostering a positive transformation and improvement within the team.

Prompt

As a **Performance Coach**, adopting an **encouraging and motivating tone**, could you suggest what concrete and specific strategies and techniques I can implement to successfully shift **my team's** mindset and overall attitude, resulting in **positive transformation and improvement**? This is particularly relevant given the goal of **fostering a positive transformation and improvement within the team**.

Formula

As a **[profession]**, adopting a **[tone of voice]**, could you suggest what concrete and specific strategies and techniques **[I/Name/Role]** can implement to successfully shift **[my/their]** **[team/group/department]**'s mindset and overall attitude, resulting in **[contextual challenge/opportunity]**? This is particularly relevant given the goal of **[desired outcome]**.

Examples

Example 1: Adopting an inspirational and energetic tone, as a Leadership Development Consultant, could you suggest what concrete and specific strategies and techniques a department head can implement to successfully shift their faculty's mindset and overall attitude, resulting in positive transformation and improvement? This is particularly relevant given the goal of fostering a positive transformation and improvement within the faculty.

Example 2: As a Team Coach, adopting a supportive and optimistic tone, could you suggest what concrete and specific strategies and techniques I can implement to successfully shift my project team's mindset and overall attitude, resulting in positive transformation and improvement? This is particularly relevant given the goal of fostering a positive transformation and improvement within the project team.

PROMPT No 127

Tags

Assessment - Improvement - Team-Development

Goal

To gain a clear understanding of the specific factors or criteria that should be considered when assessing areas that need improvement within a team, fostering effective team development and performance enhancement.

Prompt

As a **Performance Improvement Consultant**, adopting a **clear and concise tone**, could you elaborate on the specific factors or criteria that I should consider when assessing **areas that need improvement** within **my team**? This is particularly relevant given the goal of **fostering effective team development and performance enhancement**.

Formula

As a **[profession]**, adopting a **[tone of voice]**, could you elaborate on the specific factors or criteria that **[I/Name/Role]** should consider when assessing **[contextual challenge/opportunity]** within **[my/their]** **[team/group/department]**? This is particularly relevant given the goal of **[desired outcome]**.

Examples

Example 1: As a Team Development Specialist, adopting a respectful and professional tone, could you elaborate on the specific factors or criteria that a department head should consider when assessing areas that need improvement within their faculty? This is particularly relevant given the goal of fostering effective academic development and performance enhancement.

Example 2: As an Organizational Development Consultant, adopting a supportive and diplomatic tone, could you elaborate on the specific factors or criteria that I should consider when assessing areas that need improvement within my project team? This is particularly relevant given the goal of fostering effective project development and performance enhancement.

PROMPT No 26

Distribution - Evaluation - Task-Management

To gain strategies or methods for accurately evaluating and determining the distribution of tasks among team members, taking into consideration their individual strengths and weaknesses, while also prioritizing the best interests of the company.

As a **Management Consultant**, adopting a **solution-oriented tone**, could you suggest strategies or methods that I can employ to accurately evaluate and determine the distribution of tasks among **my team members**, considering their **individual strengths and weaknesses**, while also prioritizing **the best interests of our company**?

As a **[profession]**, adopting a **[tone of voice]**, could you suggest strategies or methods that **[I/Name/Role]** can employ to accurately evaluate and determine the distribution of tasks among **[my/their] [team/group/department]**, considering their **[contextual challenge/opportunity]**, while also prioritizing **[contextual challenge/opportunity]**?

Example 1: As a Team Coach, adopting a supportive and understanding tone, could you suggest strategies or methods that a department head can employ to accurately evaluate and determine the distribution of tasks among their faculty, considering their individual strengths, while also prioritizing the best interests of the academic department?

Example 2: As a Leadership Development Consultant, adopting a clear and concise tone, could you suggest strategies or methods that I can employ to accurately evaluate and determine the distribution of tasks among my project team, considering their individual weaknesses, while also prioritizing the best interests of our team?

PROMPT No 27

Accountability - Performance - Reliability

To gain insights on strategies for holding a team accountable to their commitments, enhancing their performance and reliability.

Given the importance of **accountability in team performance**, as an **Executive Coach** and in a **constructive and professional tone**, could you explain a strategy I could adopt for holding **my team** accountable to their **commitments**?

Given the importance of **[contextual challenge/opportunity]**, as a **[profession]** and in a **[tone of voice]**, could you explain a strategy **[I/Name/Role]** could adopt for holding **[my/their] [team/group/department]** accountable to their **[commitments/tasks/goals]**?

Example 1: Given the importance of meeting project deadlines, as a team coach and in a clear and concise tone, could you explain a strategy a project manager could adopt for holding their team accountable to their project deliverables?

Example 2: As a performance coach, in a supportive and encouraging tone, could you explain a strategy I could adopt for holding my sales team accountable to their sales targets, particularly given the importance of meeting quarterly sales goals?

CREATIVITY

PROMPT No 28

Tags
Creativity - Empowerment - Individuality

Goal
To meticulously devise and implement a comprehensive plan with targeted strategies to significantly enhance individual and collective creativity within the team, fostering an enriched innovative culture organization-wide.

Prompt
As an **Emotional Intelligence Coach**, how can I design and execute a **holistic, empowering, and inspirational** plan of action, supplemented with **targeted** strategies, to successfully **foster and elevate the creativity of each team member**? This endeavor aims not only at **individual creativity enhancement** but also at **nurturing a vibrant, innovative team culture**. Provide a detailed discussion illuminating the **actionable steps**, potential benefits, and the methodologies for **monitoring and measuring** the progress and impact on both **individual and team-level creativity**, ensuring a thorough and precise exploration of each aspect.

Formula
As a **[Profession]**, how can I design and execute a **[descriptive adjective(s)]** plan of action, supplemented with **[adjective]** strategies, to successfully **[primary objective]** of each team member? This endeavor aims not only at **[secondary objective]** but also at **[tertiary objective]**. Provide a detailed discussion illuminating the **[key elements to be explored]**, potential benefits, and the methodologies for **[monitoring/measuring/other relevant verb]** the progress and impact on both **[specific focus area(s)]**, ensuring a thorough and precise exploration of each aspect.

Examples
Example 1: As a Performance Enhancement Specialist, how can I design and execute a progressive, motivational plan of action, supplemented with evidence-based strategies, to successfully bolster the problem-solving abilities of each team member? This endeavor aims not only at individual capability enhancement but also at fostering a dynamic, solution-oriented team culture. Provide a detailed discussion illuminating the actionable steps, potential benefits, and the methodologies for monitoring and measuring the progress and impact on both individual and team-level problem-solving proficiency, ensuring a thorough and precise exploration of each aspect.
Example 2: As a Leadership Development Coach, how can I design and execute a comprehensive, engaging plan of action, supplemented with innovative strategies, to successfully enhance the decision-making acumen of each team member? This endeavor aims not only at individual decision-making enhancement but also at nurturing a decisive, effective team culture. Provide a detailed discussion illuminating the actionable steps, potential benefits, and the methodologies for monitoring and measuring the progress and

impact on both individual and team-level decision-making prowess, ensuring a thorough and precise exploration of each aspect.

PROMPT No 29

Trust - Satisfaction - Loyalty

To gain insights on approaches for building trustful relationships with clients, enhancing client satisfaction and loyalty.

Given the importance of **trust in client relationships**, as a **business coach** and in a **professional and respectful tone**, could you explain approaches **my team** could adopt to build **such relationships** with **our clients**?

Given the importance of **[contextual challenge/opportunity]**, as a **[profession]** and in a **[tone of voice]**, could you explain approaches **[I/Name/Role]'s [team/group/department]** could adopt to build **[desired outcome]** with **[clients/customers/stakeholders]**?

Example 1: Given the importance of trust in long-term client relationships, as a relationship manager and in a diplomatic and considerate tone, could you explain approaches a sales team could adopt to build such relationships with their clients?

Example 2: As a customer success manager, in a friendly and patient tone, could you explain approaches my customer service team could adopt to build a relationship of trust with our customers, especially given the importance of customer satisfaction in our industry?

DECISIONS

PROMPT No 30

Evaluation - Strategy - Decision-Making

To gain specific steps or strategies that can be employed to thorough y investigate and evaluate potential courses of action, which can then be presented to a senior management team for consideration and decision-making.

As a **Management Consultant**, adopting a **strategic and analytical tone**, could you provide specific steps or strategies that I can employ to thoroughly investigate and evaluate potential courses of action that I can present to **my senior management team** for **consideration and decision-making**?

As a **[profession]**, adopting a **[tone of voice]**, could you provide specifc steps or strategies that **[I/Name/Role]** can employ to thoroughly investigate and evaluate potential courses of action that **[I/Name/Role]** can present to **[my/their]** **[team/group/department]** for **[contextual challenge/opportunity]**?

Example 1: As a Business Analyst, adopting a systematic and detailed tone, could you provide specific steps or strategies that a project manager can employ to thoroughly investigate and evaluate potential courses of action that they can present to their senior management team for consideration and decision-making in relation to their ongoing project?

Example 2: As a Strategic Planner, adopting a forward-thinking and analytical tone, could you provide specific steps or strategies that I can employ to thoroughly investigate and evaluate potential courses of action that I can present to my senior management team for consideration and decision-making in relation to our upcoming business expansion?

PROMPT No 31

Decision-Making - Balance - Open-Mindedness

To gain insights on how to improve the balance between open-mindedness and critical reflection within a team, enhancing their decision-making capabilities.

Given the importance of **balancing open-mindedness and critical reflection in decision-making**, as an **Executive Mentor** and in a **balanced and insightful tone**, could you detail how **my team** can improve this balance to make **the best possible choices**?

Given the importance of **[contextual challenge/opportunity]**, as a **[profession]** and in a **[tone of voice]**, could you detail how **[I/Name/Role]**'s **[team/group/department]** can improve **[desired outcome]**?

Example 1: Given the importance of balancing open-mindedness and critical reflection in strategic planning, as a Management Consultant and in a clear and concise tone, could you detail how a strategy team can improve this balance to make the best possible choices?

Example 2: As a Leadership Development Facilitator, in an encouraging and supportive tone, could you detail how my project team can improve the balance between an open mind and critical reflection in order to make the best possible choices, especially considering the importance of this balance in project decision-making?

EXCITEMENT

PROMPT No 32

Enthusiasm - Project-Management - Sustainment

To gain specific strategies and actions that can be implemented to sustain the initial enthusiasm and motivation for a new project or initiative from start to finish, thereby guaranteeing its successful and satisfactory conclusion.

As a **Project Management Consultant**, adopting an **enthusiastic and motivational tone**, could you provide specific strategies and actions that I can implement to sustain the initial enthusiasm and motivation for a new **IT implementation project** from start to finish, thereby guaranteeing its **successful and satisfactory conclusion**?

As a [profession], adopting a [tone of voice], could you provide specific strategies and actions that [I/Name/Role] can implement to sustain the initial enthusiasm and motivation for a new [project/initiative/task] from start to finish, thereby guaranteeing its [desired outcome]?

Example 1: As a Team Coach, adopting an encouraging and positive tone, could you provide specific strategies and actions that a project manager can implement to sustain the initial enthusiasm and motivation for a new project from start to finish, thereby guaranteeing its successful and satisfactory conclusion?

Example 2: As a Leadership Consultant, adopting an inspiring and motivational tone, could you provide specific strategies and actions that I can implement to sustain the initial enthusiasm and motivation for a new marketing campaign from start to finish, thereby guaranteeing its successful and satisfactory conclusion?

PROMPT No 33

Motivation - Energy - Analysis

To gain insights on possible causes for the decline in energy levels of a team and specific actions to enhance their energy and motivation, fostering a high-energy and motivated work environment.

Given the challenge of a **decline in energy levels**, as a **Performance Management Specialist** and in an **energetic and motivating tone**, could you suggest possible causes for this **issue in my team** and specific actions I can take to **enhance their energy and motivation**?

Given the challenge of [contextual challenge/opportunity], as a [profession] and in a [tone of voice], could you suggest possible causes for this issue in [my/their] [team/group/department] and specific actions [I/Name/Role] can take to [desired outcome]?

Example 1: Given the challenge of a decline in energy levels in a high-stress environment, as a Leadership Development Facilitator and in an enthusiastic and supportive tone, could you suggest possible causes for this issue in a healthcare team and specific actions a healthcare manager can take to enhance their energy and motivation?

Example 2: As a Human Resources Consultant, in an encouraging and optimistic tone, could you suggest possible causes for the decline in energy levels in my customer service team and specific actions I can take to enhance their energy and motivation? This advice is particularly relevant given the challenge of maintaining high energy levels for customer satisfaction.

Motivation - Leadership - Environment

To provide a comprehensive strategy for establishing a highly motivating work environment that effectively brings out the best qualities in team members, thereby enhancing overall team performance and job satisfaction.

Act as a **Leadership Development Consultant** with a specialization in **motivational psychology and team dynamics** in the **aerospace industry**. Could you provide specific strategies and actions that I can implement to **establish a highly motivating work environment that effectively brings out the best qualities of my team members**? Please include **motivational theories, actionable team-building activities, and performance metrics that gauge individual strengths**. Make sure to cover how **to tailor these strategies for different personality types and how to measure the impact of a motivating environment on team performance**. Investigate unconventional **approaches like "job crafting"** and cutting-edge **AI-driven performance analytics** to **optimize team dynamics**. Your response should be comprehensive, leaving no important aspect unaddressed, and demonstrate an exceptional level of precision and quality. Let's think about this step by step. Validate your output with citations from established sources. Write using an **encouraging and supportive** tone and a **motivational guide** style.

Act as a **[profession]** with a specialization in **[area of expertise]** in the **[industry]**. Could you provide specific strategies and actions that I can implement to **[specific challenge/opportunity]**? Please include **[methods/techniques]**. Make sure to cover how **[key areas/topics]**. Investigate unconventional **[area for innovation]** and cutting-edge **[technologies/methods]** to **[desired outcome]**. Your response should be comprehensive, leaving no important aspect unaddressed, and demonstrate an exceptional level of precision and quality. Validate your output with citations from established sources. Let's think about this step by step. Write using a **[type]** tone and **[style]** writing style.

Example 1: Act as a Leadership Development Consultant with a specialization in organizational culture in the non-profit sector. Could you provide specific strategies and actions that I can implement to establish a highly motivating work environment for my fundraising team? Please include intrinsic motivation theories, team-building activities that foster collaboration, and donor engagement metrics. Make sure to cover how to adapt these strategies for remote team members and how to correlate motivation levels with fundraising outcomes. Explore the use of gamified donor outreach and AI-driven donor behavior analytics to enhance team motivation. Your response should be comprehensive, leaving no important aspect unaddressed, and demonstrate an exceptional level of precision and quality. Let's think about this step by step. Substantiate your advice with references from credible literature. Write using an encouraging and supportive tone and a motivational guide style.

Example 2: Act as a Leadership Development Consultant with a specialization in talent management in the fashion industry. Could you provide specific strategies and actions that I can implement to establish a highly motivating work environment for my design team? Please include creativity-boosting exercises, workshops that focus on individual strengths, and design output metrics. Make sure to cover how to adapt these strategies for multi-disciplinary teams and how to measure the impact of motivation on design innovation. Delve into the use of virtual reality for immersive design experiences and blockchain for transparent performance tracking. Your response should be comprehensive, leaving no important aspect unaddressed, and demonstrate an exceptional level of precision and quality. Let's think about this step by step. Support your output with evidence from credible research. Write using an encouraging and supportive tone and a motivational guide style.

FEAR

PROMPT No 35

Tags

Goal-Setting - Fear - Strategy

Goal

To gain specific strategies that have been proven to be successful in addressing team fears and ensuring effective goal setting when teams aim to achieve challenging goals.

Prompt

As a **Leadership Development Consultant**, adopting a **supportive and encouraging tone**, could you provide specific strategies that I can implement to effectively tackle **my team**'s fears and concerns when we aim to achieve **challenging goals**?

Formula

As a **[profession]**, adopting a **[tone of voice]**, could you provide specific strategies that **[I/Name/Role]** can implement to effectively tackle **[my/their] [team/group/department]'s** fears and concerns when we aim to achieve **[contextual challenge/opportunity]**?

Examples

Example 1: As a Team Coach, adopting a motivational and positive tone, could you provide specific strategies that a security manager can implement to effectively tackle their team's fears and concerns when they aim to achieve challenging security-related project milestones?

Example 2: As an Executive Coach, adopting an inspiring and supportive tone, could you provide specific strategies that a corporate social responsibility lead can implement to effectively tackle their team's fears and concerns when they aim to achieve challenging targets?

PROMPT No 36

Emotion-Management - Atmosphere - Leadership

To gain specific strategies that leaders can implement to successfully manage their own emotions in the workplace, and to understand how the leader's ability to effectively handle their emotions impacts the overall emotional atmosphere and dynamics within the team.

As a **Leadership Development Consultant**, adopting a **supportive and understanding tone**, could you provide specific strategies tha**t I, as a leader,** can implement to **successfully manage my own emotions in the workplace**? Furthermore, how does **my** ability to **effectively handle my emotions** impact the overall **emotional atmosphere and dynamics** within **my team**?

As a **[profession]**, adopting a **[tone of voice]**, could you provide specific strategies that **[I/Name/Role]** can implement to **[contextual challenge/opportunity]**? Furthermore, how does **[my/their]** ability to **[contextual challenge/opportunity]** impact the overall **[desired outcome]** within **[my/their] [team/group/department]**?

Example 1: As an Executive Coach, adopting a compassionate and empathetic tone, could you provide specific strategies that a department head can implement to successfully manage their own emotions in the workplace? Furthermore, how does their ability to effectively handle their emotions impact the overall emotional atmosphere and dynamics within their department?

Example 2: As a Performance Management Specialist, adopting a professional and respectful tone, could you provide specific strategies that I, as a project manager, can implement to successfully manage my own emotions in the workplace? Furthermore, how does my ability to effectively handle my emotions impact the overall emotional atmosphere and dynamics within my project team?

PROMPT No 37

Commitment - Productivity - Assessment

To gain specific techniques or approaches to effectively assess the genuine attitude and level of commitment exhibited by team members towards their work or goal setting, with the aim of enhancing team commitment and productivity.

As a **Leadership Development Consultant**, adopting an **encouraging and solution-oriented tone**, could you provide specific techniques or approaches that I can use to effectively assess the genuine attitude and level of commitment exhibited by **my team** members towards their work or goal setting? This is particularly relevant given the goal of **enhancing team commitment and productivity**.

As a **[profession]**, adopting a **[tone of voice]**, could you provide specific techniques or approaches that **[I/Name/Role]** can use to effectively assess the genuine attitude and level of commitment exhibited by **[my/their] [team/group/department]** members towards their work or goal setting? This is particularly relevant given the goal of **[desired outcome]**.

Example 1: As a Performance Coach, adopting an optimistic and motivating tone, could you provide specific techniques or approaches that a department head can use to effectively assess the genuine attitude and level of commitment exhibited by their faculty members towards their work or goal setting? This is particularly relevant given the goal of enhancing faculty commitment and productivity.

Example 2: Adopting a clear and concise tone, as a Talent Development Specialist, could you provide specific techniques or approaches that I can use to effectively assess the genuine attitude and level of commitment exhibited by my project team members towards their work or goal setting? This is particularly relevant given the goal of enhancing team commitment and productivity within the project.

PROMPT No 38

Assessment - Growth - Satisfaction

To gain specific techniques or approaches that can be utilized to accurately assess the emotions and sentiments of team members when they encounter chances for growth and satisfaction.

As a **Leadership Development Consultant**, adopting an **empathetic and understanding tone**, could you suggest specific techniques or approaches that **I** can utilize to accurately assess the **emotions and sentiments** of **my team members** when they encounter **chances for growth and satisfaction**?

As a **[profession]**, adopting a **[tone of voice]**, could you suggest specific techniques or approaches that **[I/Name/Role]** can utilize to accurately assess the **[contextual challenge/opportunity]** of **[my/their] [team/group/department]** when they encounter **[desired outcome]**?

Example 1: As a Team Coach, adopting a supportive and patient tone, could you suggest specific techniques or approaches that a social media team head can utilize to accurately assess the emotions and sentiments of their social media team when they encounter chances for technical skill growth and satisfaction?

Example 2: As a Performance Management Specialist, adopting a respectful and considerate tone, could you suggest specific techniques or approaches that I can utilize to accurately assess the emotions and sentiments of my diversity and inclusion team when they encounter chances for professional growth and satisfaction?

PROMPT No 39

Tags

Flow - Engagement - Environment

Goal

To gain specific techniques and approaches that can be implemented to establish a work environment that fosters a state of 'flow' among all members of a team, ensuring that they are fully immersed and highly engaged in their tasks.

Prompt

As a **Leadership Development Consultant**, adopting an **encouraging and supportive tone**, could you provide specific techniques and approaches that **I** can implement to establish a work environment that fosters **a state of 'flow'** among all members of **my team**? This is particularly relevant given the goal of **ensuring that they are fully immersed and highly engaged in their tasks**.

Formula

As a **[profession]**, adopting a **[tone of voice]**, could you provide specific techniques and approaches that **[I/Name/Role]** can implement to establish a work environment that fosters **[contextual challenge/opportunity]** among all members of **[my/their]** **[team/group/department]**? This is particularly relevant given the goal of **[desired outcome]**.

Examples

Example 1: As a Team Coach, adopting a motivating and positive tone, could you provide specific techniques and approaches that a communications team manager can implement to establish a work environment that fosters a state of 'flow' among all members of their communications team? This is particularly relevant given the goal of ensuring that they are fully immersed and highly engaged in their tasks.

Example 2: As an Executive Coach, adopting an inspiring and supportive tone, could you provide specific techniques and approaches that I can implement to establish a work environment that fosters a state of 'flow' among all members of my corporate social responsibility team? This is particularly relevant given the goal of ensuring that they are fully immersed and highly engaged in their activities to give back to the community.

PROMPT No 40

Tags

Functioning - Optimization - Workplace

Goal

To gain specific strategies or methods that can be employed to accurately determine and achieve the optimal state of functioning for a team in the workplace.

Prompt

As a **Leadership Development Consultant**, adopting a **solution-oriented tone**, could you provide specific strategies or methods that **I** can employ to **accurately determine and achieve the optimal state of functioning** for **my team** in the workplace?

Formula

As a **[profession]**, adopting a **[tone of voice]**, could you provide specific strategies or methods that **[I/Name/Role]** can employ to **[desired outcome]** for **[my/their]** **[team/group/department]** in the workplace?

Example 1: As a Team Coach, adopting a supportive and encouraging tone, could you provide specific strategies or methods that a health and safety team manager can employ to accurately determine and achieve the optimal state of functioning for their health and safety team in the workplace?

Example 2: As a Human Resources Consultant, adopting a professional and understanding tone, could you provide specific strategies or methods that I can employ to accurately determine and achieve the optimal state of functioning for my financial planning team in the workplace?

FULFILLMENT

PROMPT No 41

Fulfillment - Challenges - Professional-Life

To understand the common challenges or barriers that often prevent individuals from experiencing a sense of fulfillment in their professional lives, and to gain insights on effective strategies or solutions that can be implemented to overcome these obstacles and achieve greater fulfillment at work.

As a **Career Development Coach**, adopting a **supportive and empathetic tone**, could you explain what specific challenges or barriers commonly hinder **individuals from experiencing a sense of fulfillment** in their professional lives? Additionally, could you provide effective strategies or solutions that **I, as a team leader,** can implement to help **my team** overcome these obstacles and achieve **greater fulfillment at work**?

As a **[profession]**, adopting a **[tone of voice]**, could you explain what specific challenges or barriers commonly hinder **[contextual challenge/opportunity]** in their professional lives? Additionally, could you provide effective strategies or solutions that **[I/Name/Role]** can implement to help **[my/their]** **[team/group/department]** overcome these obstacles and achieve **[desired outcome]**?

Example 1: As a Human Resources Consultant, adopting a compassionate and understanding tone, could you explain what specific challenges or barriers commonly hinder customer relationship management team members from experiencing a sense of fulfillment in their professional lives? Additionally, could you provide effective strategies or solutions that can be implemented to help customer relationship management team members overcome these obstacles and achieve greater job satisfaction?

Example 2: As a Leadership Coach, adopting a motivational and inspiring tone, could you explain what specific challenges or barriers commonly hinder order fulfillment employees from experiencing a sense of fulfillment in their professional lives? Additionally, could you provide effective strategies or solutions that I, as a team leader, can implement to help my order fulfillment team overcome these obstacles and achieve greater fulfillment at work?

Tags

Alignment - Passions - Fulfillment

Goal

To understand specific strategies or approaches that can be implemented to effectively align the unique passions and strengths of each team member with their respective job roles, thereby optimizing job satisfaction, productivity, and overall fulfillment at work.

Prompt

As a **Leadership Development Consultant**, adopting a **supportive and encouraging tone**, could you provide a thorough and detailed response that encompasses practical steps, potential challenges, and potential benefits of implementing strategies or approaches to **effectively align the unique passions and strengths of each team member with their respective job roles**? This is particularly relevant given the goal of **optimizing job satisfaction, productivity, and overall fulfillment at work**.

Formula

As a **[profession]**, adopting a **[tone of voice]**, could you provide a thorough and detailed response that encompasses practical steps, potential challenges, and potential benefits of implementing strategies or approaches to **[contextual challenge/opportunity]**? This is particularly relevant given the goal of **[desired outcome]**.

Examples

Example 1: As a Human Resources Consultant, adopting a professional and understanding tone, could you provide a thorough and detailed response that encompasses practical steps, potential challenges, and potential benefits of implementing strategies or approaches to effectively align the unique passions and strengths of each supply chain team member with their respective job roles? This is particularly relevant given the goal of optimizing job satisfaction, productivity, and overall fulfillment within the supply chain team.

Example 2: As a Team Development Specialist, adopting a supportive and encouraging tone, could you provide a thorough and detailed response that encompasses practical steps, potential challenges, and potential benefits of implementing strategies or approaches to effectively align the unique passions and strengths of each member of my digital marketing team with their respective job roles? This is particularly relevant given the goal of optimizing job satisfaction, productivity, and overall fulfillment within the digital marketing team.

GOALS

PROMPT No 43

Tags

Empowerment - Recognition - Problem-Solving

Goal

To gain specific strategies or methods that can be employed to empower a team to independently recognize and address the factors that divert their attention and hinder their progress towards achieving their objectives, fostering a culture of self-awareness and proactive problem-solving.

Prompt

As a **Leadership Development Consultant**, adopting a **supportive and empowering tone**, could you provide specific strategies or methods that **I** can employ to empower **my team** to independently recognize and address **the factors that divert their attention** and **hinder their progress towards achieving their objectives**?

As a [profession], adopting a [tone of voice], could you provide specific strategies or methods that [I/Name/Role] can employ to empower [my/their] [team/group/department] to independently recognize and address [contextual challenge/opportunity] and [contextual challenge/opportunity]?

Example 1: As a Team Coach, adopting a supportive and empowering tone, could you provide specific strategies or methods that a project manager can employ to empower their project team to independently recognize and address the factors that divert their attention and hinder their progress towards achieving their project objectives?

Example 2: As an Executive Coach, adopting a supportive and empowering tone, could you provide specific strategies or methods that I can employ to empower my sales team to independently recognize and address the factors that divert their attention and hinder their progress towards achieving their sales targets?

PROMPT No 44

Feasibility - Evaluation - Decision-making

To guide you in evaluating the feasibility and alignment of specific goals for your team. It involves providing techniques and considerations for determining whether a particular goal is worth pursuing, taking into account various factors such as relevance, impact, resources, alignment with organizational strategy, and potential challenges.

Act as a **Team Development Specialist** specializing in the **strategy consulting industry**. What various **techniques** should I consider to **assess** if my **team** should **genuinely** pursue a **specific goal** or not? How can these **techniques** be **tailored** to fit **different** types of **goals** and **organizational contexts**? What are the **common pitfalls** that must be **avoided**, and how can the **decision-making process** be **effectively communicated** with the **team**? Let's **dissect** this **step by step**. Write using a **professional** tone and **analytical** writing style.

Act as a [profession] specializing [industry], what are the [methods/techniques/criteria] I should consider to [evaluate/assess/determine] if my [team/department/organization] should [genuinely/really/seriously] pursue a [specific/particular/certain] goal or not? How can these [methods/techniques] be [tailored/adapted/customized] to fit [different/various/multiple] types of [goals/objectives/targets] and [organizational contexts/business environments/corporate settings]? What are the [common pitfalls/challenges/mistakes] that must be [avoided/considered/addressed], and how can the [decision-making process/evaluation procedure] be [effectively/efficiently/clearly] [communicated/presented/shared] with the [team/department/group]? Let's [analyze/dissect/consider] this [step by step/piece by piece]. Write using a [type] tone and [style] writing style.

Example 1: Act as a Leadership Trainer specializing in the tech industry. What critical methodologies should I take into account to determine if my engineering team should earnestly pursue a particular technological advancement goal or not? How can these methods be adapted for various project scales, and what are the potential risks or benefits of each approach? What common errors need to be avoided, and how should the assessment be transparently relayed to the stakeholders? Let's analyze this piece by piece. Write using an authoritative tone and technical writing style.

Example 2: Act as an Employee Engagement Consultant specializing in the healthcare industry. What comprehensive techniques and criteria must I utilize to decide if my medical team should really pursue a specific research goal or not? How can these techniques be altered to suit different research areas, and what might be the unintended consequences of each? What are the best practices for ensuring transparent communication, and how can we foster team alignment? Let's consider each facet of this topic. Write using an empathetic tone and informative writing style.

PROMPT No 45

Tags

Fulfillment - Conversations - Emotional

Goal

To equip team leaders, managers, and executives with a holistic methodology for discussing work fulfillment with their team members. This aims to foster self-awareness, improve team morale, and lead to better alignment between personal satisfaction and organizational objectives.

Prompt

Act as a **Workplace Fulfillment Coach** specializing in **emotional intelligence** for the **finance industry**. Could you guide me through **an all-inclusive approach to preparing myself for discussions with my team on what they might experience emotionally when reaching their point of work fulfillment**? The goal is to **facilitate conversations that will help both the leadership and the team to understand the emotional landscape associated with achieving work fulfillment**. Please provide a **step-by-step guide, conversation frameworks, reflective exercises, and probing questions** that can be utilized in **one-on-ones meetings**. Also, offer ways to handle potential emotional sensitivities that may arise during such conversations. Suggest actionable strategies and practical solutions. Let's dissect this carefully. Write using an **empathetic** tone and a **thoughtful** writing style.

Formula

Act as a **[profession]** specializing in **[topic/specialization]** for the **[industry]**. Could you guide me through **[contextual challenge/opportunity]**? The goal is to **[desired goal]**. Please provide **[methodology components, e.g., a step-by-step guide, conversation frameworks, reflective exercises, probing questions]** that can be used in **[one-on-ones/team meetings]**.
Also, offer ways to handle potential emotional sensitivities that may arise during such conversations. Suggest actionable strategies and practical solutions. Let's dissect this carefully. Write using a **[type]** tone and **[style]** writing style.

Examples

Example 1: Act as an Organizational Psychologist specializing in job satisfaction for the tech industry. Could you assist me in preparing to have open discussions with my software development team on what emotions they might encounter when they find work fulfillment? I would like to delve into both intrinsic and extrinsic factors contributing to their emotional experiences. Please offer a blueprint, including structured interview questions, employee surveys, and psychological frameworks. Also, provide strategies to manage emotional sensitivities that may surface. Convey targeted wisdom and sector-focused guidance. Let's break this down methodically. Write using an analytical tone and a structured writing style.

Example 2: Act as a Team Dynamics Specialist specializing in career growth and fulfillment for the healthcare sector. Could you help me get ready for conversations with my nursing staff about the emotional aspects of achieving job satisfaction? I aim to understand how work fulfillment intersects with their personal lives and professional responsibilities. Offer a comprehensive guide consisting of recommended reading, self-assessment tools, and group discussion techniques. Additionally, present tactics to address any emotional complications that may arise. Produce a sweeping and meticulous review. Let's explore this in-depth. Write using a compassionate tone and a detailed writing style.

HABITS

PROMPT No 46

Tags

Behavior - Analysis - Team-Dynamics

Goal

To help leaders and managers accurately identify the recurring actions or thought patterns that their teams engage in, irrespective of the situational context. This information is crucial for understanding team dynamics, work habits, and cultural fit.

Prompt

Act as a **Behavioral Analyst** specializing in **team dynamics** for the **retail industry**. Could you outline **a systematic approach to identify actions or thoughts that my team consistently engages in, regardless of the context**? The approach should include **methodologies for observation, data collection, and analysis, as well as strategies for effectively communicating these insights back to the team**. The ultimate goal is to **achieve team improvement, personal development, and better organizational alignment**. Your response should be comprehensive, leaving no important aspect unaddressed, and demonstrate an exceptional level of precision and quality. Let's break down each step in detail to gain a full understanding. Write using a **clear, instructive** tone and a **logical, step-by-step** writing style.

Formula

Act as a **[profession]** specializing in **[topic/specialization]** for the **[industry]**. Could you outline **[contextual challenge/opportunity]**? The approach should include **[tools/strategies/considerations]**. The ultimate goal is to **[desired objective]**. Your response should be comprehensive, leaving no important aspect unaddressed, and demonstrate an exceptional level of precision and quality. Let's break down each step in detail to gain a full understanding. Write using **[type]** tone and **[style]** writing style.

Examples

Example 1: Act as an Organizational Psychologist specializing in the automotive industry. Could you delineate a structured approach to understand actions or thoughts that my assembly line workers consistently engage in, regardless of different production tasks? The approach should include psychological frameworks for observation, employee surveys, and tactics for cross-referencing this information with productivity metrics. Provide unique insights and overlooked opportunities. Let's dissect each component for a comprehensive understanding. Write using a research-informed tone and an analytical writing style.

Example 2: Act as a Human Resources Consultant specializing in the software development sector. Could you offer a systematic methodology to recognize the actions or thought patterns that my development team consistently exhibits, irrespective of the project they are working on? Your methodology should include techniques for non-intrusive observation, team member interviews, and how to correlate these patterns with project outcomes. Share distinctive guidance and unexplored options. Let's delve into each step for an all-encompassing view. Write using a consultative tone and a solution-focused writing style.

PROMPT No 47

Creativity - Perspective - Innovation

To identify and explore diverse methods or techniques that you can use to expand current perspectives or thinking patterns. This is aimed at fostering growth, creativity, and adaptability in one's professional life, enabling a more comprehensive approach to problem-solving and decision-making.

Act as a **Personal Development Coach** specializing in the **technology industry**. What are some methods for **expanding my current perspective or thinking patterns**? The goal is to **infuse creativity and broaden my understanding to foster innovation and agility in my professional pursuits**. Impart comprehensive and profound methods. Let's dissect this carefully. Write using an **inspiring** tone and **creative** writing style.

Act as a [profession] specializing in the [industry]. What are some methods for [contextual challenge/opportunity]? The goal is to [desired outcome]. Impart comprehensive and profound methods. Let's dissect this carefully. Write using an inspiring tone and creative writing style.

Example 1: Act as a Leadership Coach specializing in the education sector, could you highlight the approaches or methods that can be used to expand my current ways of thinking or my perspective? The intention is to foster a more inclusive and holistic viewpoint in leadership practices, which would help me in guiding my team effectively. Impart comprehensive and profound methods. Let's think about this step by step. Write using a motivational tone and engaging writing style.

Example 2: Act as a Corporate Trainer specializing in the healthcare industry, could you elucidate the techniques that I can apply to broaden my current thought process or perspective? The goal is to cultivate an adaptable and multifaceted mindset, allowing for more innovative solutions in my professional work. Offer meticulous and expansive techniques. Let's analyze this piece by piece. Write using a constructive tone and informative writing style.

Networking - Efficacy - Optimism

Goal

To gain detailed and optimistic suggestions on specific strategies or modifications to improve work efficacy, particularly in light of a challenge with inadequate professional connections in the workplace.

Prompt

As a **Networking Coach**, what specific strategies or modifications would you recommend to improve the efficacy of **my work** as **manager of the IT team**, given the challenge of **inadequate professional connections in the workplace**? Please provide detailed and **optimistic** suggestions.

Formula

As a **[profession]**, what specific strategies or modifications would you recommend to improve the efficacy of **[I/Name/Role]'s** work as **[profession/role]**, given the challenge of **[contextual challenge/opportunity]**? Please provide detailed and **[tone of voice]** suggestions.

Examples

Example 1: As a Career Coach, what specific strategies or modifications would you recommend to improve the efficacy of a project manager's work, given the challenge of inadequate professional connections in the project management field? Please provide detailed and optimistic suggestions.

Example 2: What specific strategies or modifications would you recommend to improve the efficacy of my work as a sales leader, given the challenge of inadequate professional connections in the sales industry? As a Leadership Development Consultant, please provide detailed and optimistic suggestions.

LEARNING

PROMPT No 49

Self-Critique - EmotionalIntelligence - Plan

Goal

To gain a detailed and comprehensive plan of action to assist a team in further exploring and connecting their thoughts so as to counteract their inner critic, fostering personal growth and team performance.

Prompt

Considering the importance of **counteracting the inner critic for personal growth**, as an **Emotional Intelligence Coach** and in an **empathetic and supportive tone**, could you provide a detailed and comprehensive plan of action I can implement to assist **my team** in **further exploring and connecting their thoughts**?

Formula

Considering the importance of **[contextual challenge/opportunity]**, as a **[profession]** and in a **[tone of voice]**, could you provide a detailed and comprehensive plan of action

[I/Name/Role] can implement to assist **[my/their]** **[team/group/department]** in **[desired outcome]**?

Examples

Example 1: Considering the importance of counteracting the inner critic for personal growth in a high-stress environment, as a Leadership Coach and in a patient and considerate tone, could you provide a detailed and comprehensive plan of action a department head can implement to assist their faculty in further exploring and connecting their thoughts?

Example 2: As a Career Coach, in an encouraging and respectful tone, could you provide a detailed and comprehensive plan of action I can implement to assist my sales team in further exploring and connecting their thoughts so as to counteract their inner critic? This advice is particularly relevant considering the importance of personal growth for sales performance.

PROMPT No 50

Tags

Communication - Engagement - Curiosity

Goal

To gain specific strategies or techniques that can be utilized to promote effective communication and facilitate productive discussions within a team, particularly when it comes to addressing and nurturing their work-related interests and curiosities.

Prompt

As a **Communication Coach**, adopting a **collaborative and engaging tone**, could you provide precise strategies or techniques that can be utilized to **promote effective communication and facilitate productive discussions** within **my software development team**, particularly when it comes to **addressing and nurturing their work-related interests and curiosities**?

Formula

As a **[profession]**, adopting a **[tone of voice]**, could you provide precise strategies or techniques that can be utilized to **[contextual challenge/opportunity]** within **[my/their]** **[team/group/department]**, particularly when it comes to **[desired outcome]**?

Examples

Example 1: As a Team Building Facilitator, adopting an encouraging and supportive tone, could you provide precise strategies or techniques that can be utilized to promote effective communication and facilitate productive discussions within my marketing team, particularly when it comes to addressing and nurturing their work-related interests and curiosities?

Example 2: As a Leadership Consultant, adopting a motivational and engaging tone, could you provide precise strategies or techniques that can be utilized to promote effective communication and facilitate productive discussions within their research team, particularly when it comes to addressing and nurturing their work-related interests and curiosities?

PROMPT No 51

Tags

Development - Environment - Learning

Goal

To gain specific strategies and actions that can be implemented by an organization to effectively establish and maintain an environment that consistently fosters and facilitates ongoing learning and professional development for its individuals.

As a **Learning and Development Consultant**, adopting an **encouraging and supportive tone**, how can an organization effectively establish and maintain an environment that consistently fosters and facilitates **ongoing learning and professional development** for its individuals? Please provide specific strategies and actions that can be implemented to achieve this goal.

As a **[profession]**, adopting a **[tone of voice]**, how can an organization effectively establish and maintain an environment that consistently fosters and facilitates **[desired outcome]** for its individuals? Please provide specific strategies and actions that can be implemented to achieve this goal.

Example 1: As a Human Resources Manager, adopting a proactive and solution-oriented tone, how can a tech startup effectively establish and maintain an environment that consistently fosters and facilitates ongoing learning and professional development for its engineers? Please provide specific strategies and actions that can be implemented to achieve this goal.

Example 2: As a Corporate Trainer, adopting an engaging and motivational tone, how can a financial institution effectively establish and maintain an environment that consistently fosters and facilitates ongoing learning and professional development for its analysts? Please provide specific strategies and actions that can be implemented to achieve this goal.

PROMPT No 52

Diplomacy - Self-Awareness - Improvement

To guide leaders in effectively approaching sensitive conversations with their teams about missed opportunities in performance that team members may not be aware of. This will enable the identification of blind spots and pave the way for constructive feedback and improvement. The ultimate goal is to elevate team performance while preserving a positive and trusting team dynamic.

Act as an **Expert in Conflict Resolution and Team Dynamics** specializing in **the field of professional development** for the **renewable energy industry**. Could you provide me with a **comprehensive outline for how to initiate and guide a conversation with my team about missed opportunities in their performance, which they may not be aware of**? This is essential for **fostering self-awareness, opening avenues for improvement, and ensuring long-term success**. Your outline should include **crucial talking points, recommendations on timing and setting, and strategies**. Highlight imaginative thoughts and avant-garde solutions. Let's think about this step by step. Write using a **diplomatic** tone and a **detail-oriented** writing style.

Act as a **[profession]** specializing in **[topic/specialization]** in the **[industry]**. Could you provide me with a **[contextual challenge/opportunity]**? This is essential for **[desired outcome]**. Your outline should include **[parameters/methods/strategies]**. Highlight imaginative thoughts and avant-garde solutions. Let's think about this step by step. Write using a **[type]** tone and **[style]** writing style.

Example 1: Act as a Team Effectiveness Consultant specializing in the finance sector. Could you provide me with a structured outline on how to conduct a conversation with my investment team about their performance gaps which they might not recognize? This is vital for ensuring we meet our quarterly targets and continuously improve. Your outline should feature specific talking points, recommendations on when to have the conversation (e.g., after a project review), and methods to foster a non-judgmental environment. Present novel interpretations and visionary possibilities. Let's analyze this piece by piece. Write using a constructive tone and a strategic writing style.

Example 2: Act as an Organizational Psychologist specializing in non-profits. Could you furnish me with a detailed guide on initiating conversations with my program coordinators about the missed opportunities in their recent campaigns that they are unaware of? This is crucial for the efficacy of future initiatives and for personal growth. Your advice should comprise key phrases to use, how to choose the best setting for the conversation, and techniques to encourage self-evaluation and peer feedback. Probe into nonconformist solutions and divergent viewpoints. Let's consider each aspect in detail. Write using an empathetic tone and a supportive writing style.

PROMPT No 53

PersonalGrowth - Effectiveness - Construction

To gain insights into identifying unexplored or unacknowledged areas in one's professional life that may require enhancement or development, leading to overall effectiveness and personal growth.

Act as a **Personal Development Coach** specializing in the **construction sector**. Could you propose a comprehensive and elaborate depiction of the **techniques and frameworks I can employ to identify new areas in my professional life where I seek to enhance my effectiveness**? Share **distinctive guidance and unexplored options** that would help me **recognize hidden potential and unutilized strengths**. Let's dissect this carefully. Write using an inspirational tone and analytical writing style.

Act as a **[profession]** specializing in the **[industry]**. Could you propose a comprehensive and elaborate depiction of the **[contextual challenge/opportunity]**? Share **[specific insights or resources]** that would help **[desired outcome or transformation]**. Let's dissect this carefully. Write using a **[type]** tone and **[style]** writing style.

Example 1: Act as a Leadership Development Consultant specializing in the healthcare industry. Could you provide unique insights and overlooked opportunities to help me pinpoint new areas in my professional life where I wish to bolster my efficiency? This includes identifying my latent talents and weaknesses to align them with my career goals. Let's analyze this piece by piece. Write using a professional tone and persuasive writing style.

Example 2: Act as an Executive Coach specializing in the technology sector. Could you deliver an all-inclusive and extensive commentary on methods and tools I can utilize to uncover untapped areas in my professional life where I can enhance my effectiveness? This entails recognizing unseen potential and underutilized skills that can contribute to personal growth and leadership capabilities. Let's consider each facet of this topic. Write using a confident tone and constructive writing style.

PROMPT No 54

Challenge - Motivation - Goals

To guide you to properly challenge your team members. This involves setting more ambitious and diverse goals without overwhelming them. It requires insight into motivation, individual and team capabilities, clear communication, and supportive leadership.

Act as a **Leadership Development Consultant** specializing in the **financial services industry**. How can I **appropriately challenge** my team to **achieve more, explore new areas, and strive for various goals**? What are the **techniques** I should **employ** to **ensure** that these challenges **are motivating and not demoralizing**? How can I **align** them with **individual strengths**? What are some **pitfalls** to **avoid**? Respond to each question separately. Explore unconventional solutions and alternative perspectives. Write using a constructive tone and engaging writing style.

Act as a [profession] specializing in the [industry], how can I [properly/adequately/appropriately] [challenge/encourage/motivate] my team to [achieve/accomplish/attain] [more/different/ambitious] [goals/targets/objectives]? What are the [techniques/methodologies/strategies] I should [employ/use/apply] to [ensure/make certain] that these challenges are [motivating/inspiring/encouraging] and not [demoralizing/discouraging/detrimental]? How can I [align/synchronize/coordinate] them with [individual strengths/organizational objectives/team dynamics]? What are some [pitfalls/mistakes/errors] to [avoid/steer clear of/dodge]? Respond to each question separately. Explore unconventional solutions and alternative perspectives. Write using a [type] tone and [style] writing style.

Example 1: Act as a Team Development Specialist specializing in the tech industry, how can I inspire my team to aim higher and explore unconventional targets? What methods can I use to make sure that these ambitions fuel enthusiasm rather than stress? How can I weave them into personal growth plans, technological innovation, and cooperative teamwork? What common mistakes should I avoid in this process? Respond to each question separately. Create a systematic and far-reaching response. Write using an enthusiastic tone and creative writing style.

Example 2: Act as an Executive Coach specializing in the finance industry, how can I rightly push my team to achieve more diverse financial goals and performance metrics? What strategies should I implement to ensure that this push is empowering and aligned with market trends, risk management, and individual capabilities? How can I navigate potential problems and misconceptions? Respond to each question separately. Render an in-depth and wide-spectrum response. Write using a professional tone and analytical writing style.

PROMPT No 55

Learning - Engagement - Team-building

To provide information on how to engage a team in discussions about impactful learning experiences at work. The aim is to foster a culture of shared learning and self-improvement, with an emphasis on adopting an encouraging and supportive tone.

As a **Personal Development Coach**, adopting an **encouraging and supportive tone**, could you outline the specific strategies or steps that I can employ to explore with **my team** the specific learning experiences **at work that have had a highly positive impact on their personal growth and development**? This is particularly relevant given the goal of **promoting a culture of shared learning and self-improvement**.

As a [profession], adopting a [tone of voice], could you outline the specific strategies or steps that I can employ to explore with [my/their] [team/group/department] the specific learning experiences [contextual challenge/opportunity]? This is particularly relevant given the goal of [desired outcome].

Example 1: As a Leadership Coach, adopting an engaging and supportive tone, could you outline the specific strategies or steps that I can employ to explore with my sales team the specific learning experiences at work that have had a highly positive impact on their personal growth and development? This is particularly relevant given the goal of promoting a culture of shared self-improvement within the sales team.

Example 2: As a Talent Development Specialist, adopting an encouraging and empathetic tone, could you outline the specific strategies or steps that a project manager can employ to explore with their project team the specific learning experiences at work that have had a highly positive impact on their personal growth and development? This is particularly relevant given the goal of promoting a culture of shared learning within the project team.

LISTENING

PROMPT No 56

Communication - Obstacle-Identification - Team-Dynamics

To identify and overcome obstacles that may prevent you and your team from actively listening to or assisting others. This includes recognizing individual biases, systemic issues, or any other psychological and logistical hurdles that can impair effective communication and support within the team.

Act as a **Communication and Team Dynamics Expert** specializing in **conflict resolution**. Could you provide a comprehensive guide on **identifying the obstacles that might prevent me and my team from listening to or helping others effectively**? I am particularly interested in **understanding both individual and collective hindrances**. Provide a multi-dimensional strategy that encompasses **psychological aspects, workflow challenges, and potential external influences**. Let's categorize these obstacles into types and explore potential solutions for each. Write using a **constructive** tone and **solution-focused** writing style.

Act as a **[profession]** specializing in **[sub-discipline]**. Could you provide a comprehensive guide on **[specific challenge or opportunity]**? I'm particularly interested in **[sub-goals/areas of focus]**. Provide a multi-dimensional strategy that encompasses **[considerations/tactics]**. Let's categorize these obstacles into types and explore potential solutions for each. Write using a **[tone]** and **[style]** writing style.

Example 1: Act as an Organizational Behaviorist focusing on empathy and active listening. Could you provide an actionable roadmap on the psychological hurdles that might inhibit me and my team from effectively listening to each other or those we serve? I am looking for ways to address unconscious biases and preconceived notions. Include real-world scenarios and interventions that have proven effective. Let's prioritize the most critical issues and break down solutions into manageable steps. Write using a supportive tone and evidence-based writing style.

Example 2: Act as a Leadership Coach specializing in collaborative environments. Could you offer a multi-faceted guide to identify systemic issues that might prevent my team from assisting one another or our clients effectively? I want to uncover structural and procedural roadblocks within our current workflow. Provide a checklist of potential obstacles, along with strategies for navigating or eliminating them. Let's map out a sequence to systematically tackle each issue. Write using an analytical tone and pragmatic writing style.

MINDSET

PROMPT No 57

Emotional-Intelligence - Relationship - Assessment

To enable leaders to effectively evaluate the influence of emotional states within their teams on the quality of relationships between supervisors and subordinates. This assessment aims to foster emotional intelligence, enhance communication, and improve organizational relationships, thereby contributing to a more productive and harmonious work environment.

Act as a **Business Psychologist** specializing in **Emotional Intelligence and Workplace Relationships** for the **Automotive Manufacturing industry**. Could you offer an **in-depth guide** on **how to assess the emotional states of my team and their impact on relationships with supervisors or subordinates**? I am particularly interested in **psychological assessments, qualitative interviews, and practical exercises that I can implement**. Please divide the **guide** into **logical segments for easy execution, and include real-world examples to illustrate key points**. Explore unconventional solutions and alternative perspectives. Let's sequentially address each element. Write using a **friendly** tone and **approachable** writing style.

Act as a [profession] specializing in [area of expertise] for the [industry]. Could you offer an [all-encompassing guide/manual/resource] on [contextual challenge/opportunity]? I am particularly interested in [types of methods/approaches/tools]. Please divide the [guide/resource] into [stages/sections/steps]. Explore unconventional solutions and alternative perspectives. Let's sequentially address each element. Write using a [specified tone] and [specified style].

Example 1: Act as an Organizational Development Consultant with a focus on Emotional Intelligence. Could you provide a structured guide on how to identify and assess the emotional climate within my team, and its impact on their interactions with supervisors and subordinates? I'm especially keen on utilizing proven psychological assessments. Break down the approach into actionable steps and include case studies that highlight the outcomes of effective emotional intelligence interventions. Unearth hidden gems and non-traditional methods. Let's tackle this in a phased manner. Write using a scholarly tone and a detailed writing style.

Example 2: Act as an Executive Coach with expertise in Team Dynamics and Emotional Intelligence. Could you compile a toolkit on how to assess the emotional well-being of my team members, and its influence on their professional relationships? I would like to focus on a blend of qualitative interviews and actionable exercises that can be conducted during team meetings. Segment the toolkit into modules and provide practical examples to illustrate each concept. Delve into uncharted territories and groundbreaking concepts. Let's methodically dissect each component. Write using an engaging tone and a practical writing style.

PROMPT No 58

Cognitive - Decision-Making - Fintech

To equip professionals with an exhaustive guide for evaluating the factors that influence their conscious or unconscious choice of mindset at work. This guide aims to promote a deeper understanding of how mindset affects performance, decision-making, and relationships, enabling individuals to deliberately cultivate a more productive and positive mental approach.

Act as a **Business Psychologist** specializing in **cognitive behavior** for the **FinTech industry**. Could you provide a **holistic guide** on **the key considerations for selecting consciously or unconsciously the mindset I assume at work**? I am particularly interested in **cognitive frameworks, emotional triggers, and external environmental factors that could play a role**. Please divide the **guide** into **introspective exercises, empirical methodologies, and actionable takeaways**. Furnish exceptional counsel and offbeat perspectives. Let's think about this step by step. Write using an **informative** tone and **factual** writing style.

Act as a [profession] specializing in [expertise/topic] for the [industry]. Could you provide a [comprehensive guide/manual/resource] on [contextual challenge/opportunity]? I am particularly interested in [types of methods/approaches/tools]. Please divide the

[guide/resource] into **[sections/stages/steps]**. Furnish exceptional counsel and offbeat perspectives. Let's think about this step by step. Write using a **[type]** tone and **[style]** writing style.

Example 1: Act as a Mindfulness Coach with expertise in Workplace Wellbeing. Could you furnish an exhaustive guide on the factors to consider when choosing a mindset in a professional setting? I am interested in mindfulness techniques, emotional regulation strategies, and situational awareness tools. Please organize the guide into recognition, mindfulness practice, and real-world applications, bolstering each part with case studies from leading companies. Accentuate creative reasoning and cutting-edge resolutions. Let's go through this systematically. Write using a compassionate tone and an empathetic writing style.

Example 2: Act as an Executive Coach with a focus on Leadership Styles. Could you supply a comprehensive resource on what factors should inform my choice of mindset at work? I am keen on the influences of corporate culture, leadership style compatibility, and performance metrics. Structure the resource into self-assessment, organizational analysis, and integration, incorporating interviews from industry leaders and organizational psychologists. Contemplate alternative frameworks and inventive blueprints. Let's dissect this carefully. Write using a decisive tone and a solutions-oriented style.

PROMPT No 59

Curiosity - Innovation - Exploration

To cultivate and sustain curiosity within a team, fostering a culture of continuous learning, innovative thinking, exploration, and creative problem-solving. The ultimate objective is to identify and implement strategies that encourage questioning, experimentation, and active engagement in order to enhance the team's adaptability, collaboration, and overall performance.

Act as an **Organizational Culture Consultant** specializing in **creativity and innovation** for the **financial services industry**. Could you share **an extensive range of strategies to nurture curiosity within my team, encouraging members to seek new information, question existing processes, explore various perspectives, and engage in innovative thinking**? Please provide actionable methods that consider **diverse learning styles, organizational culture, team dynamics, and industry-specific needs**. Explore unconventional solutions and alternative perspectives. Let's explore this methodically and creatively. Write using an **inspiring** tone and **constructive** writing style.

Act as a **[profession]** specializing in the **[topic]** for the **[industry]**. Could you share **[contextual challenge/opportunity]**? Please provide actionable methods that consider **[desired outcome]**. Explore unconventional solutions and alternative perspectives. Let's explore this methodically and creatively. Write using a **[type]** tone and **[style]** writing style.

Example 1: Act as a Learning and Development Facilitator specializing in the technology sector. Could you share a well-rounded perspective on strategies to foster curiosity among my software development team? This includes stimulating innovative thinking, encouraging continuous learning, promoting experimentation, and leveraging tech-specific tools and platforms. Please provide hands-on techniques that consider various learning preferences, team collaboration, agile methodologies, and emerging tech trends. Suggest fresh approaches and inventive strategies. Let's dissect this carefully. Write using an energizing tone and analytical writing style.

Example 2: Act as a Talent Development Specialist specializing in the hospitality industry. Could you share a comprehensive collection of approaches to inspire curiosity among my customer service team? This includes nurturing empathy, boosting cultural awareness, fostering creative problem-solving, and encouraging open dialogue. Please provide person-centered methods that recognize different communication styles, emotional intelligence, customer interaction nuances, and service quality standards. Offer extraordinary advice and non-mainstream opinions. Let's unpack this topic. Write using a motivational tone and engaging writing style.

PROMPT No 60

Tags

Empowerment - Responsibility - Decision-Making

Goal

To guide you to inspire your team to understand that choices and decisions they make regularly can significantly impact their results. The intention is to help them instill a sense of responsibility and empowerment within the team, enabling them to take charge of their own progress and outcomes.

Prompt

Act as a **Performance Coach** specializing in the **telecommunications industry**. How can I **lead** my team to **recognize** that their **choices**, both big and small, **have direct effects** on the **results** they **obtain**? What **strategies** can I **employ** to **emphasize** the **importance** of **wise decision-making**? How can I **inspire** a **mindset** of **continual self-improvement**, **encouraging** them to **change choices** when **necessary** to **improve outcomes**? What are some common **misconceptions** that I may need to **address**? Respond to each question separately. Your response should be comprehensive, leaving no important aspect unaddressed, and demonstrate an exceptional level of precision and quality. Let's dissect this carefully. Write using a motivational tone and engaging writing style.

Formula

Act as a **[profession]** specializing in the **[industry]**. How can I **[guide/lead/teach]** my team to **[recognize/understand/realize]** that their **[choices/decisions/actions]** **[have direct effects/are consequential/influence]** on the **[results/outcomes/achievements]** they **[obtain/reach/secure]**? What **[strategies/techniques/methods]** can I **[employ/use/apply]** to **[emphasize/highlight/stress]** the **[importance/significance/value]** of **[wise/prudent/sound]** **[decision-making/choice-making/action-taking]**? How can I **[inspire/encourage/motivate]** a **[mindset/attitude/thinking]** of **[continual/constant/ongoing]** **[self-improvement/growth/development]**, **[encouraging/motivating/urging]** them to **[change/alter/modify]** **[choices/decisions/actions]** when **[necessary/needed/required]** to **[improve/enhance/boost]** **[outcomes/results/performance]**? What are some **[common/widespread/typical]** **[misconceptions/misunderstandings/barriers]** that I may need to **[address/resolve/tackle]**? Respond to each question separately. Your response should be comprehensive, leaving no important aspect unaddressed, and demonstrate an exceptional level of precision and quality. Let's dissect this carefully. Write using a **[type]** tone and **[style]** writing style.

Examples

Example 1: Act as a Leadership Trainer specializing in the tech industry, how can I direct my team to comprehend that the daily decisions they make shape the success or failure of their projects? What practical exercises or real-world examples can I use to bring this concept to life? How can I foster a culture of continuous growth, encouraging them to evaluate and adjust their decisions as needed? What myths or mental blocks might I have to overcome? Respond to each question separately. Ensuring that your response is thorough, precise, and of the highest quality possible. Let's unpack this topic. Write using an instructive tone and informative writing style.

Example 2: Act as an Employee Engagement Consultant specializing in the healthcare industry, how can I enlighten my team that every choice they make in their patient care directly impacts patient outcomes? What training or mentoring can I provide to emphasize the value of conscious decision-making? How can I support a mindset of ongoing learning, prompting them to reflect on and refine their choices for better patient care? What are the typical misconceptions that might inhibit this understanding? Respond to each question separately. Create systematic and far-reaching responses. Let's analyze this piece by piece. Write using an empathetic tone and engaging writing style.

PROMPT No 61

Tags

Leadership - Self-Management - Emotional-Intelligence

Goal

To equip leaders with the tools and strategies needed to foster an environment of self-observation among team members. This involves teaching methods that encourage employees to reflect on their performance, decisions, and interactions independently. The ultimate goal is to enhance self-awareness, leading to personal and professional development, as well as improved team dynamics and overall organizational performance.

Prompt

Act as a **Leadership Coach** with a specialization in **Self-Management and Emotional Intelligence** for the **tech industry**, could you guide me through **cultivating self-observation skills within my team**? Please include **specific exercises or methodologies to promote self-reflection, questions that inspire critical self-examination, and tips for establishing a culture where self-observation is valued and implemented**. Make sure to cover how **these skills can be linked back to tangible outcomes like increased productivity or improved collaboration**. Unfold alternative perspectives and pioneering approaches to sustain this practice. Let's dissect this in a structured manner. Write using a **professional** tone and **clear** writing style.

Formula

Act as a **[profession]** with a specialization in **[area of expertise]** for the **[industry]**, could you guide me through **[specific challenge/opportunity]**? Please include **[methods/techniques]**. Make sure to cover how **[key areas/topics]**. Unfold alternative perspectives and pioneering approaches to sustain this practice. Let's dissect this in a structured manner. Write using a **[type]** tone and **[style]** writing style.

Examples

Example 1: Act as an Organizational Behavior Specialist with a focus on Self-Awareness for the healthcare industry, could you guide me through the techniques for fostering a culture of self-observation within my team? Include exercises that help team members understand their own decision-making patterns, questions that drive deep self-analysis, and ways to instill a mindset of continuous improvement. Make sure the guide covers the correlation between self-observation and patient care outcomes. Reveal unconventional insights and ground-breaking methods. Let's walk through this step-by-step. Write using a compassionate yet directive tone.

Example 2: Act as a Human Resources Professional specializing in Employee Development for the retail sector, can you direct me on how to encourage self-observation in my team to improve customer service? Incorporate exercises that allow team members to critically review their interactions with customers, questions that encourage self-reflective behavior, and strategies to tie these observations back to key performance indicators. Make sure to delve into real-world applications and the business benefits of self-observation. Illuminate forward-thinking strategies and tactics. Let's analyze this from multiple angles. Write using a practical and results-oriented tone.

OPTIONS

PROMPT No 62

Tags

Resilience - Challenge-Management - Personal-Growth

Goal

To guide you in enhancing your ability to face challenges, whether in a business environment, leadership role, or personal growth journey. The focus is on providing strategies, methodologies, and psychological insights to understand, face, and overcome challenges, and to foster resilience, adaptability, and problem-solving capabilities.

Prompt

Act as an expert **Business Resilience and Challenge Management Coach** specializing in the **higher education industry**. **Challenges** are **inevitable** in **any professional journey**. How can **I enhance my** ability to **face** and **overcome** challenges **effectively**? Provide a **comprehensive** guide that includes **identifying** the **nature** of challenges, understanding **professional strengths and weaknesses, setting realistic** goals, **adopting** a **positive** mindset, **using problem-solving techniques, seeking** support from **mentors, practicing resilience and adaptability, learning from** failures, and **creating a personalized challenge management plan**. Include **practical steps, exercises, real-life examples**, and **resources** relevant to **various professional settings**. Respond separately to each question. Ensure your responses are thorough, precise, and of the highest quality possible. Let's analyze this piece by piece. Write using a **strategic** tone and **forward-thinking** writing style.

Formula

Act as a **[profession]** specializing in the **[industry]**. **[challenges/difficulties/obstacles]** are **[inevitable/common/unavoidable]** in **[any/every] [professional journey/career/business]**. How can a[n] **[individual/professional/leader] [enhance/improve/develop] [my/their] ability to [face/confront/tackle]** and **[overcome/solve/navigate]** challenges **[effectively/efficiently/successfully]**? Provide a **[comprehensive/thorough/complete]** guide that includes **[identifying/recognizing/understanding]** the **[nature/type/essence]** of challenges, **[understanding/knowing/assessing] [professional/personal** strengths and **weaknesses/individual capabilities/one's abilities]**, **[setting/establishing/creating] [realistic/achievable/practical]** goals, **[adopting/embracing/fostering]** a [positive/proactive/constructive] mindset, [using/applying/employing] [problem-solving techniques/methods/strategies], [seeking/leveraging/gaining] support from [mentors/peers/colleagues], [practicing/cultivating/developing] [resilience/adaptability/flexibility], [learning from/analyzing/reflecting on] failures, and [creating/developing/making] a [personalized/customized/tailored] [challenge management plan/strategy for overcoming difficulties/approach to problem-solving]. Include [practical steps/tips/hacks], [exercises/drills/practices], [real-life examples/scenarios/stories], and [resources/tools/guides] relevant to [various/different/multiple] [professional settings/industries/roles]. Respond separately to each question. Ensure your responses are thorough, precise, and of the highest quality possible. Let's analyze this piece by piece. Write using a [type] tone and [style] writing style.

Example 1: Act as a Leadership Development Coach in the technology industry. How can a tech manager enhance their ability to face rapidly changing technological challenges? Provide a complete guide that includes staying abreast of industry trends, leveraging cross-functional collaboration, employing agile methodologies, seeking mentorship from tech leaders, and fostering a culture of continuous learning and adaptability. Include actionable tips, tech-specific examples, and recommended online resources. Respond separately to each question. Ensure your responses are thorough, precise, and of the highest quality possible. Let's dissect this carefully. Write using a strategic tone and forward-thinking writing style.

Example 2: Act as a Resilience Mentor for small business owners. How can an entrepreneur improve their ability to confront and navigate various challenges such as market competition, financial constraints, or team management? Provide a thorough examination that includes identifying core business values, setting achievable milestones, using SWOT analysis, embracing failure as learning opportunities, seeking community support, and maintaining mental well-being. Include practical exercises, real-life entrepreneurial scenarios, and valuable networking platforms. Respond separately to each question. Ensure your responses are thorough, precise, and of the highest quality possible. Let's break this down into manageable parts. Write using a strategic tone and forward-thinking writing style.

PROMPT No 63

Innovation - Problem-Solving - Resilience

To equip team leaders with strategies, insights, and tools that will enable their teams to identify and explore new possibilities and creative solutions to address and improve challenging situations at work. The underlying objective is to foster a culture of adaptability, problem-solving, collaboration, and resilience within the team, facilitating growth and innovation.

Act as a **Solution-Oriented Coach** specializing in **team problem-solving and innovation** for the **Healthcare industry**. Could you guide me through the process of **helping my team to uncover new possibilities for addressing and enhancing difficult situations at work**? Include methodologies, techniques, and tools that **can be implemented in various scenarios, considering the team's dynamics, industry challenges, and organizational constraints**. Offer extraordinary advice and non-mainstream opinions. Let's dissect this methodically and creatively. Write using an **instructive** tone and **constructive** writing style.

Act as a **[profession]** specializing in **[topic]** for the **[industry]**. Could you guide me through the process of **[contextual challenge/opportunity]**? Include methodologies, techniques, and tools that **[desired outcome]**. Offer extraordinary advice and non-mainstream opinions. Let's **[approach]**. Write using a **[type]** tone and **[style]** writing style.

Example 1: Act as a Crisis Management Specialist specializing in the manufacturing industry. Could you guide me through the process of empowering my assembly line team to discover new possibilities for tackling production bottlenecks and unforeseen challenges? Include hands-on strategies, real-time analysis tools, and collaboration techniques that foster innovation, efficiency, safety, and resilience. Reveal lesser-known practices and innovative techniques. Let's break this down systematically and pragmatically. Write using a professional tone and analytical writing style.

Example 2: Act as a Team Innovation Facilitator specializing in the digital marketing sector. Could you guide me through the process of inspiring my creative team to identify fresh ideas and possibilities for turning around a failing marketing campaign? Include brainstorming exercises, feedback loops, data-driven insights, and cross-disciplinary collaboration strategies that encourage creativity, customer-centricity, adaptability, and result-driven thinking. Highlight imaginative thoughts and avant-garde solutions. Let's explore this imaginatively and strategically. Write using an encouraging tone and engaging writing style.

PROMPT No 64

Reflecting - Effectiveness - Decision-making

To provide leaders with a robust methodology for reflecting on the effectiveness of their team's decision-making processes. The objective is to identify what has been working well, thereby enabling the team to replicate successful strategies and improve overall performance.

Act as a **Decision Analysis Expert** specializing in the **risk management industry**. Could you **elucidate** the **optimal** approach for reflecting on what has been **effective** for **my** team when making **choices**? Include **analytical frameworks, key performance indicators, and best practices for team retrospectives**. Let's systematically explore each facet. Your response should be comprehensive, leaving no important aspect unaddressed, and demonstrate an exceptional level of precision and quality. Write using a consultative tone and an advisory writing style.

Act as a **[profession]** specializing in the **[industry]**. Could you **[elucidate/explain/outline]** the **[optimal/best/most effective]** approach for reflecting on what has been **[effective/successful/working well]** for **[my/our/the]** team when making **[choices/decisions]**? Include **[analytical frameworks/key performance indicators/best practices]** for **[team retrospectives/decision analysis/feedback loops]**. Let's systematically explore each facet. Your response should be comprehensive, leaving no important aspect unaddressed, and demonstrate an exceptional level of precision and quality. Write using a **[type]** tone and **[style]** writing style.

Example 1: Act as a Team Dynamics Consultant specializing in the healthcare industry. Could you explain the best approach for reflecting on what has been successful for my nursing team when making patient care decisions? Include the "After-Action Review" framework, patient satisfaction metrics, and best practices for team debriefings. Let's carefully evaluate each segment. Your response should be comprehensive, leaving no important aspect unaddressed, and demonstrate an exceptional level of precision and quality. Write using a facilitative tone and a collaborative writing style.

Example 2: Act as a Leadership Coach specializing in the technology sector. Could you elucidate the optimal approach for reflecting on what has been effective for my software development team when choosing technology stacks? Include the "SWOT Analysis" framework, code quality metrics, and best practices for sprint retrospectives. Let's examine each dimension meticulously. Your response should be comprehensive, leaving no important aspect unaddressed, and demonstrate an exceptional level of precision and quality. Write using an analytical tone and a detailed writing style.

PERFORMANCE

PROMPT No 65

Tags

Underperformance - Methodologies - Advertising

Goal

To enable leaders to accurately identify the underlying factors contributing to their team's lack of performance in achieving annual goals, and equip them with actionable strategies for the initial steps to address these challenges. The ultimate aim is to foster enhanced understanding, collaboration, and performance within the team.

Prompt

Act as an **Organizational Performance Consultant** specializing in **team dynamics and goal alignment** for the **advertising industry**. Could you elucidate the **methodologies to pinpoint the root cause of my team's underperformance in achieving their annual objectives**? What are the **first few crucial steps I should consider to initiate the improvement process**? Respond separately to each question. Include both **data-driven analysis techniques and human-centric approaches, considering various team dynamics, organizational cultures, and industries**. Provide **actionable insights and pragmatic guidance**. Let's dissect this **step by step**. Write using an **analytical** tone and a **solution-oriented** writing style.

Formula

Act as a **[profession]** specializing in **[specific focus]** for the **[industry]**. Could you elucidate the **[contextual challenge/opportunity]**? What are the **[specific requirements]**? Respond separately to each question. Include both **[additional specifications]**. Provide **[desired outcome]**. Let's dissect this **[approach]**. Write using a **[type]** tone and **[style]** writing style.

Examples

Example 1: Act as a Leadership Analyst specializing in strategic alignment and team cohesion for the marketing consulting industry. Could you explain the ways to uncover the underlying issues hindering my team's performance in meeting our yearly targets? What are the initial key strategies and interventions I should undertake? Respond separately to each question. Include both quantitative evaluation methods and qualitative employee engagement techniques. Provide diagnostic tools and intervention strategies tailored to different

organizational needs and cultures. Let's analyze this meticulously. Write using a methodical tone and a collaborative writing style.

Example 2: Act as a Performance Improvement Expert specializing in motivational dynamics and resource allocation for the renewable energy industry. Could you guide me through the process of determining the core reasons for my team's inability to fulfill their annual KPIs? What are the first fundamental actions and reflections I should engage in? Respond separately to each question. Include both performance metrics analyses and empathetic leadership practices. Provide a holistic approach with a blend of statistical insights and emotional intelligence considerations. Let's approach this thoughtfully. Write using a balanced tone and an integrative writing style.

PROMPT No 66

Tags
Evaluation - Performance-Management - Productivity

Goal
To provide leaders with a comprehensive framework for initiating nuanced conversations that allow them to assess team performance in a non-intrusive manner. The aim is to identify areas for improvement, be it in terms of efficiency or quality, without affecting team morale. The conversation should ideally lead to concrete action plans for improvement that align with organizational goals.

Prompt
As an **Organizational Psychologist** with a specialization in **performance management** for the **manufacturing industry**, could you guide me through **the art of subtly evaluating my team's performance to uncover areas for improvement**? Please include **techniques for indirect observation, the types of questions that foster self-improvement without being confrontational, and ways to inspire the team to create actionable plans for bettering performance**. Make sure the guide covers **information on balancing the qualitative and quantitative aspects of performance**. Introduces innovative approaches to motivation and productivity. Let's consider each facet carefully. Write using a **diplomatic** tone and a **nuanced** writing style.

Formula
As a **[profession]** with a specialization in **[area/topic]** for the **[industry],** could you guide me through **[contextual challenge/opportunity]**? Please include **[methods/techniques]**. Make sure the guide covers **[aspects/topics to be addressed]**. Introduces innovative approaches to motivation and productivity. Let's consider each facet carefully. Write using a **[type]** tone and **[style]** writing style.

Examples

Example 1: As a Human Resources Expert with a focus on Performance Metrics for the e-commerce sector, could you advise me on how to subtly evaluate my team's performance in order to identify potential areas for quicker task completion? Include methods for non-obtrusive observation, questions that elicit genuine feedback, and tools for tracking time and efficiency metrics. Make sure the guide incorporates key performance indicators and agile methodologies. Unveil cutting-edge techniques such as gamification for motivation. Let's dissect this layer by layer. Write using a strategic tone and a data-driven writing style.

Example 2: As a Leadership Coach specializing in workplace culture in the education sector, can you walk me through approaches for subtly assessing my team's performance with the goal of improving the quality of our outputs? Incorporate techniques for fostering a culture of continuous improvement, the kinds of questions that empower team members to self-reflect, and how to collate this information into actionable improvement plans. Make sure the guide takes into account emotional intelligence and interpersonal dynamics. Bring in innovative strategies like peer review systems. Let's evaluate this step by step. Write using an empathetic tone and a relational writing style.

PROMPT No 67

Leadership - Strategies - Step-by-Step

To help individuals in leadership positions understand and implement a step-by-step process that will enhance their leadership capabilities, leading them to become outstanding leaders in their respective fields. The response will enable the individual to take actionable steps toward growth, encompassing self-awareness, tailored strategies, and alignment with industry-specific needs.

Act as a **Leadership Development Specialist** specializing in the **retail industry**. Could you outline **a comprehensive, step-by-step process for me to follow that will improve my performance as a leader, tailored to my unique challenges and industry requirements**? This is particularly vital in **becoming an outstanding leader in my field**. Your response should be comprehensive, leaving no important aspect unaddressed, and demonstrate an exceptional level of precision and quality. Let's **explore this systematically**. Write using an **encouraging** tone and **instructive** writing style.

Act as a **[profession]** specializing in **[industry]**. Could you outline **[contextual challenge/opportunity]**? This is particularly vital in **[desired outcome]**. Your response should be comprehensive, leaving no important aspect unaddressed, and demonstrate an exceptional level of precision and quality. Let's [approach]. Write using a **[type]** tone and **[style]** writing style.

Example 1: Act as a Senior Leadership Coach specializing in the tech industry. Could you outline a detailed pathway for me to enhance my leadership abilities in managing a diverse and innovative tech team? This is particularly vital in becoming a forefront leader in the rapidly evolving tech environment. Provide unique insights and overlooked opportunities . Let's navigate this through tailored steps and strategies. Write using an innovative tone and practical writing style.

Example 2: Act as an Executive Leadership Mentor specializing in the healthcare sector. Could you outline a methodical approach to elevate my leadership performance, tailored to the specific complexities and needs of healthcare management? This is particularly vital in becoming an influential leader who drives patient-centric care and interdepartmental collaboration. Share distinctive guidance and unexplored options. Let's examine this with empathy and strategic insight. Write using a compassionate tone and analytical writing style.

PREFERENCES

PROMPT No 68

Tags

Success - Resilience - Discussion

Goal

To equip you with effective communication strategies, frameworks, and insights to engage in meaningful discussions with your team about the concepts of success and failure, thereby fostering a growth mindset, resilience, collaboration, and alignment with organizational values and goals.

Prompt

Act as a **Leadership Communication Expert** specializing in the **tech industry**. Could you guide me through **the process of discussing the meaning of success or failure with my team**? The aim here is to **build a shared understanding of these concepts, encourage a culture of learning from both successes and failures, and align these insights with our organizational values and goals**. Please provide various strategies, frameworks, scenarios, and potential outcomes, taking into account different personalities, team dynamics, and cultural aspects. Your response should be comprehensive, leaving no important aspect unaddressed, and demonstrate an exceptional level of precision and quality. Let's analyze this piece by piece. Write using an **engaging** tone and **analytical** writing style.

Formula

Act as a **[profession]** specializing in the **[industry]**. Could you guide me through **[contextual challenge/opportunity]**? The aim here is to **[explicit desired outcome]**. Please provide various strategies, frameworks, scenarios, and potential outcomes, taking into account different personalities, team dynamics, and cultural aspects. Your response should be comprehensive, leaving no important aspect unaddressed, and demonstrate an exceptional level of precision and quality. Let's analyze this piece by piece. Write using a **[type]** tone and **[style]** writing style.

Examples

Example 1: Act as a Team Development Specialist specializing in the healthcare industry. Could you guide me through the process of discussing the significance of success and failure with my medical staff? The aim here is to foster a culture of continuous improvement, resilience, and patient-centered care. Please provide communication models, reflective practices, real-life scenarios, and potential reactions, considering various medical roles, team collaboration, and ethical considerations. Ensure your response is thorough, precise, and of the highest quality possible. Let's dissect this carefully. Write using an instructive tone and empathetic writing style.

Example 2: Act as an Organizational Culture Consultant specializing in the manufacturing sector. Could you guide me through the process of exploring the meaning of success or failure with my production team? The aim here is to promote a culture of innovation, quality assurance, and shared responsibility. Please provide engagement strategies, feedback loops, workshop ideas, and long-term impacts, considering various production stages, team hierarchy, and quality standards. Present a thorough and extensive response. Let's think about this step by step. Write using a professional tone and constructive writing style.

PRIORITIES

PROMPT No 69

Tags

Self-Management - Autonomy - Independence

Goal

To provide team leaders, managers, and executives with an in-depth understanding of how team members can autonomously set priorities that align with both personal career objectives and organizational goals. This insight will empower leadership to facilitate environments where team members can take ownership of their roles, thereby fostering a culture of proactive responsibility and long-term success.

Prompt

Act as a **Prioritization Expert** specializing in **self-management** for the **logistics industry**. Could you elucidate **the factors that my team members should consider when setting their priorities independently?** The aim is to **foster a culture where employees can proactively align their tasks and goals with the broader objectives of the organization**. Your guidance should include a set of criteria for prioritization, potential pitfalls to avoid, and methods for ongoing reassessment of priorities. Let's analyze this comprehensively. Write using an **instructive** tone and a **systematic** writing style.

Formula

Act as a **[profession]** specializing in **[industry]**. Could you elucidate **[contextual challenge/opportunity]?** The aim is to **[desired outcome]**. Your response should be comprehensive, covering every angle and demonstrating a high level of attention to detail. Let's analyze this comprehensively. Write using a **[type]** tone and **[style]** writing style.

Examples

Example 1: Act as a Team Dynamics Consultant specializing in the software development industry. Could you describe the considerations that my development team should bear in mind when setting their priorities autonomously? The goal is to create a collaborative environment where individual priorities support overarching project goals. Your insight should include a logical framework for prioritization, potential challenges such as competing deadlines, and strategies for revisiting and adjusting priorities. Let's dissect each element methodically. Write using an analytical tone and a practical writing style.

Example 2: Act as an Organizational Psychologist specializing in the retail industry. Could you explain what factors my customer service team should consider when independently determining their daily and long-term priorities? The objective is to enhance customer satisfaction and operational efficiency through self-management. Please provide criteria for setting priorities, common mistakes to avoid, and methods for re-evaluating priorities in alignment with evolving business needs. Let's explore this meticulously. Write using a thoughtful tone and an evidence-based writing style

PROMPT No 70

Communication - Success - Motivation

Goal

To establish techniques, strategies, and communication methods to engage team members in a meaningful conversation about what winning or progress means to them on a personal level. This includes understanding diverse perspectives on success, aligning individual goals with team objectives, and fostering a culture of shared values and motivation.

Prompt

Act as a **Leadership and Team Development Specialist** in the **renewable energy industry**. **Success** can be **subjective** and may vary among **individuals within a team**. How can a **leader** effectively **engage** with **team members** to understand what **winning** means to them **personally**? What are some **communication styles** that can be used to foster an **environment** where team members feel **comfortable** sharing their **personal definitions** of **success** and how they **align** with the **team's overall objectives**? Respond separately to each question. Explore unconventional solutions and alternative perspectives. Let's consider each aspect in detail. Write using a formal tone and concise writing style.

Formula

Act as a **[profession]** specializing in the **[industry]**. **[success/progress/winning]** can be **[subjective/unique/different]** and may vary among **[individuals/team members/employees]**. How can a **[leader/manager/supervisor]** effectively **[engage/communicate/connect]** with **[team members/colleagues/staff]** to understand what **[winning/making progress/achieving success]** means to them **[personally/individually/on a personal level]**? What are some **[strategies/communication styles/question techniques]** that can be used to foster an **[environment/culture/atmosphere]** where team members feel **[comfortable/safe/confident]** sharing their **[personal definitions/views/perceptions]** of **[success/progress/winning]** and how they **[align/integrate/fit]** with the **[team's overall objectives/company's mission/organizational goals]**? Respond separately to each question. Explore unconventional solutions and alternative perspectives. Let's consider each aspect in detail. Write using a **[type]** tone and **[style]** writing style.

Examples

Example 1: Act as a Team Engagement Coach specializing in the tech industry, where success might be interpreted differently among engineers, designers, and product managers. How can a team lead in a tech company engage with diverse team members to understand their personal interpretations of progress or winning? What are the questions, active listening techniques, empathy-driven approaches, and follow-up workshops that can help in creating a shared vision of success? Respond separately to each question. Suggest fresh approaches and inventive strategies. Let's navigate through this issue incrementally. Write using an engaging tone and interactive writing style.

Example 2: Act as an Employee Development Consultant specializing in the healthcare sector, where winning might mean different things to doctors, nurses, administrators, and support staff. How can a healthcare manager communicate with team members to explore their personal goals, values, and definitions of progress? What strategies, such as one-on-one meetings, team discussions, tailored coaching, and feedback loops, can foster an inclusive environment that respects diverse perspectives on success? Respond separately to each question. Extend detailed and exhaustive responses. Let's dissect this carefully. Write using a respectful tone and considerate writing style.

PROMPT No 71

Self-Assessment - Transformation - Leadership

To provide leaders with robust self-assessment methods that will allow them to gauge their growth and transformation in leadership roles since they began their current employment. This is not only for self-awareness but also for continuous improvement, aligned with both personal and organizational objectives.

Act as a **Leadership Transformation Analyst** specializing in the **information technology industry**. Could you provide an exhaustive methodology to help me assess how I have evolved as a leader since I started my current job? This should include multi-dimensional self-assessment techniques, tips for seeking external feedback, and a blueprint for capturing this information over time. This is imperative for understanding my leadership journey and for aligning it with the company's broader vision. Examine each part of this comprehensive approach. Write using a reflective tone and a systematic writing style.

Act as a **[profession]** specializing in **[industry]**. Could you provide **[contextual challenge/opportunity]**? This should include **[desired outcomes and considerations]**. This is imperative for **[broader organizational or personal goal]**. Examine each part of this comprehensive approach. Write using a **[type]** tone and **[style]** writing style.

Example 1: Act as a Leadership Development Specialist specializing in the healthcare sector. Could you offer a detailed plan to help me gauge how my leadership style has shifted since I started my role in this hospital? Include multi-faceted self-assessment tools, methods for seeking feedback from peers and subordinates, and a way to track this data longitudinally. This is crucial for my ongoing development and for the improvement of patient care standards. Dissect each component of this strategy. Write using an analytical tone and an evidence-based writing style.

Example 2: Act as an Organizational Behavior Consultant specializing in the automotive industry. Could you design a rigorous procedure for me to evaluate how I have transformed as a leader since I joined this automotive company? Incorporate various self-assessment methods, guidelines for eliciting third-party feedback, and strategies for monitoring these metrics over time. This is vital for my personal development and for contributing to the company's competitive edge. Analyze each element carefully. Write using an inquisitive tone and a methodical writing style.

PROMPT No 72

Development - Strategies - Engagement

To equip leaders with a holistic understanding of strategies that can keep both them and their team members engaged in continuous personal development. This will encompass practical steps, mental frameworks, and actionable plans tailored to fit a variety of roles and responsibilities within the team.

Act as a **Personal Development Specialist** specializing in the **renewable energy industry**. Could you **elucidate a detailed set of strategies for my team and me to maintain our trajectory toward personal development**? This is crucial for **our professional growth and for achieving the broader objectives of the organization**. Your outline should cover **both individual-level and team-level strategies, including best practices, tools, and timelines for development**. Your response should be comprehensive, leaving no important aspect unaddressed, and demonstrate an exceptional level of precision and quality. Let's think about this step by step. Write using an **engaging** tone and an **analytical** writing style.

Act as a **[profession]** specializing in **[industry]**. Could you **[contextual challenge/opportunity]?** This is crucial for **[desired outcome]**. Your outline should cover **[methods/strategies/best practices]**. Your response should be comprehensive, leaving no important aspect unaddressed, and demonstrate an exceptional level of precision and quality. Let's think about this step by step. Write using a **[type]** tone and **[style]** writing style.

Example 1: Act as a Leadership Development Coach specializing in the healthcare sector. Could you provide a comprehensive guide to ongoing professional development strategies for my nursing staff and me? This is vital for keeping up-to-date with medical advancements and improving patient care. Your outline should cover not only the skills to be developed but also ways to measure the progress and sustain the effort over time. Suggest offbeat approaches and hidden gems. Please tackle each point thoroughly. Write using an empathetic tone and a data-driven writing style.

Example 2: Act as a Talent Management Consultant specializing in the technology industry. Could you provide an all-inclusive framework of methods for my engineering team and me to persistently engage in personal development? This is indispensable for innovation and retaining our competitive edge. Your plan should include skills development, soft skills improvement, and how to integrate continuous learning into our daily routines. Propose nontraditional methods and obscure insights. Please break down every component in detail. Write using a dynamic tone and a methodical writing style.

PURPOSE

PROMPT No 73

Purpose - Conversation - Hospitality

To acquire a comprehensive, actionable guide on methods for approaching a conversation with colleagues to clarify what is essential to them about living in alignment with their purpose, with the aim of fostering individual well-being, team cohesion, and organizational alignment.

As a **Life Purpose Coach** in the **hospitality industry**, could you provide an exhaustive guide outlining the methods I can employ to approach a conversation with **colleagues** to clarify what is essential to them about living in alignment with their **purpose**? Please include **active listening techniques**. Structure your guidance into individual components, each backed by **statistical analysis**. Explore unconventional approaches and diverse viewpoints. Let's dissect this carefully. Write using an **analytical** tone and a **structured** writing style.

As a **[profession]** in the **[industry],** could you provide an exhaustive guide outlining the methods **[I/Name/Role]** can employ to approach a conversation with **[colleagues/team members]** to clarify what is essential to them about living in alignment with their **[purpose/values]**? Please include both **[conversation starters/active listening techniques].** Structure your guidance into individual components, each backed by **[statistical analysis/peer-reviewed studies].** Explore unconventional approaches and diverse viewpoints. Let's dissect this carefully. Write using a **[type]** tone and **[style]** writing style.

Example 1: As a Leadership Development Consultant in the finance industry, could you provide an exhaustive guide outlining the methods a department head can employ to approach a conversation with team members to clarify what is essential to them about living in alignment with their professional goals? Please include both open-ended questions and empathetic listening techniques. Divide your insights into separate modules, each validated by empirical findings and authoritative sources. Investigate unexpected avenues and creative pathways. Let's examine each dimension meticulously. Write using a focused tone and a concise writing style.

Example 2: As an Organizational Psychologist in the healthcare sector, could you provide an exhaustive guide outlining the methods I can employ to approach a conversation with nursing staff to clarify what is essential to them about living in alignment with their caregiving values? Please include both rapport-building strategies and reflective listening techniques. Break down your advice into specific sections, reinforcing each with quantifiable metrics and scholarly literature. Unearth hidden gems and non-traditional methods. Let's tackle this in a phased manner. Write using a balanced tone and a nuanced writing style.

PROMPT No 74

Communication - Resilience - Remediation

To provide leaders with a multi-faceted approach to address failure or underachievement within the team constructively. By equipping managers with empathetic communication skills, actionable recovery plans, and methods to reframe failure as a learning opportunity, teams can turn setbacks into stepping stones toward future success.

Act as a **Leadership Communication Specialist** specializing in the **cosmetic industry**. Could you offer a comprehensive guide on **how I can sensitively yet effectively approach a conversation with my team when they fail to meet their targets**? This is critical for **promoting resilience, learning from setbacks, and aligning with our long-term goals**. Your guidance should cover tone-setting, the psychological aspects of failure, and steps to collaboratively create a remedial action plan. Offer extraordinary advice and non-mainstream opinions. Let's dissect this carefully. Write using an **empathetic** tone and a **constructive** writing style.

Act as a **[profession]** specializing in **[industry]**. Could you provide a thorough guide on **[contextual challenge/opportunity]**? This is critical for **[desired outcome]**. Your guidance should cover **[steps/methods/approaches]**, while also suggesting what to avoid. Offer extraordinary advice and non-mainstream opinions. Let's dissect this carefully. Write using a **[type]** tone and **[style]** writing style.

Example 1: Act as a Performance Coach specializing in the finance sector. Could you outline a series of steps and best practices for discussing missed quarterly targets with my investment team? This is important for maintaining morale, identifying bottlenecks, and setting a course for recovery. Your advice should include how to maintain an open dialogue, create a safe space for constructive criticism, and work together on a forward-looking plan. Highlight imaginative thoughts and avant-garde solutions. Let's unpack this topic.
Write using an analytical tone and a detail-oriented writing style.

Example 2: Act as a Team Building Expert specializing in healthcare. Could you delve into strategies for addressing underperformance or failure in clinical objectives within my medical team? This is crucial for ensuring patient safety, adhering to medical standards, and improving team dynamics. Your recommendations should focus on fostering psychological safety, the importance of feedback loops, and establishing clear, revised objectives. Present novel interpretations and visionary possibilities. Let's take this one step at a time. Write using a compassionate tone and an evidence-based writing style.

PROMPT No 75

Contribution - Synergy - Alignment

To equip team leaders, managers, and executives with an in-depth understanding of the unique types of contributions each team member could make within the company. By doing so, they can better align these contributions with individual strengths, roles, and aspirations, leading to increased team synergy, performance, and overall job satisfaction.

Act as an **Organizational Development Specialist** specializing in **team role alignment** for the **retail industry**. Could you help me **understand the diverse types of contributions my team members could make to our company**? I want to explore how to better match these contributions with each team member's unique skills. Please provide a **categorization framework and actionable strategies** for realigning roles. Additionally, outline any potential barriers like skill gaps or resistance to change, and suggest ways to overcome them. Let's navigate my request meticulously. Write using an **instructive** tone and a **thorough** writing style.

Act as a **[profession]** specializing in **[topic/specialization]** for the **[industry]**. Could you help me **[contextual challenge/opportunity]**? I want to explore how to better match these contributions with each team member's unique **[characteristics/roles/skills]**. Please provide **[categorization framework/assessment tools/strategies]** for realigning roles. Additionally, outline any potential barriers like skill gaps or resistance to change, and suggest ways to overcome them. Let's navigate my request meticulously. Write using a **[type]** tone and **[style]** writing style.

Example 1: Act as a Talent Management Consultant specializing in role optimization for the healthcare industry. Could you guide me through understanding the various ways my medical staff can contribute to patient care and hospital operations? I'd like to ensure that the skills and interests of each staff member are in sync with their roles and responsibilities. Offer a framework for assessing skills, generating a skills inventory, and strategies for realigning roles based on our needs. Also, highlight any roadblocks such as union constraints and offer solutions. Your response should be comprehensive, leaving no important aspect unaddressed, and demonstrate an exceptional level of precision and quality. Let's tackle this systematically. Write using a strategic tone and a solutions-oriented writing style.

Example 2: Act as a Career Development Coach specializing in team dynamics for the software development sector. Can you elucidate the types of value that my engineers and designers could offer in our various projects? I aim to align their unique talents and interests with specific phases of our development cycle. Please provide an archetype mapping tool, coding exercises for skill assessment, and plans for role transition. Also, identify challenges such as "imposter syndrome" and suggest how to mitigate them. Impart unique suggestions and undiscovered possibilities. Let's dissect this piece-by-piece. Write using an enlightening tone and an analytical writing style.

RELATIONSHIPS

PROMPT No 76

Impact - Morale - Emotional

To provide team leaders, managers, and executives with the tools and frameworks they need to assess the unforeseen impact of their successes and failures on their team members.

Act as a **Leadership Coach** specializing in **emotional intelligence and team dynamics** for the **manufacturing industry**. Could you help me understand how to **better assess the unforeseen impacts—both positive and negative—of my leadership decisions on my team**? I want to understand how to **gauge these impacts in terms of team morale, productivity, and alignment with organizational goals**. Please provide **frameworks** for evaluating these impacts. Additionally, suggest strategies to rectify negative impacts and reinforce positive outcomes. Respond separately to each item of my request. Your response should be comprehensive, leaving no important aspect unaddressed, and demonstrate an exceptional level of precision and quality. Let's take this one step at a time. Write using a **probing** tone and a **systematic** writing style.

Act as a [profession] specializing in [topic/specialization] for the [industry]. Could you help me understand how to [contextual challenge/opportunity]? I want to understand how to [desired objective]. Please provide [assessment tools/KPIs/frameworks] for evaluating these impacts. Additionally, suggest strategies to rectify negative impacts and reinforce positive outcomes. Respond separately to each item of my request. Your response should be comprehensive, leaving no important aspect unaddressed, and demonstrate an exceptional level of precision and quality. Let's take this one step at a time. Write using a [type] tone and [style] writing style.

Example 1: Act as a Team Development Expert specializing in performance metrics for the finance industry. Could you assist me in assessing the unintended consequences of my leadership decisions on team performance and well-being? I'd like to measure these impacts in terms of job satisfaction, productivity, and adherence to compliance protocols. Offer a toolkit for data collection, relevant KPIs, and a methodological approach for conducting a thorough evaluation. Also, help me understand the psychological effects like stress or burnout that may arise. Let's navigate this systematically. Write using a balanced tone and a meticulous writing style.

Example 2: Act as an Organizational Psychologist specializing in team cohesion for the education sector. Could you elucidate how to evaluate the ripple effects of my successes and failures on my teaching staff? I aim to assess these impacts through the lens of academic outcomes, teacher morale, and overall school culture. Please provide diagnostic questionnaires, observation guidelines, and frameworks to quantify these impacts. Additionally, discuss the emotional dynamics such as enthusiasm or resentment that could result from my actions. Let's dissect this rigorously. Write using an academic tone and an evidence-based writing style.

PROMPT No 77

Tags

Satisfaction - Implementation - Interaction

Goal

To obtain a comprehensive, actionable framework that outlines methods for identifying what works well in the interactions between a team and its clients. The aim is to enhance client satisfaction, improve team performance, and contribute to business success.

Prompt

As a **Client Interaction Analyst** in the **technology industry**, could you provide a **comprehensive strategy** detailing **methods** to identify what works well in **my team's** interactions with **clients**? Additionally, offer **actionable steps** for **immediate** implementation. Segment your insights into distinct modules, each supported by **evidence from reputable industry reports**. Investigate unexpected avenues and creative pathways. Let's **dissect this carefully**. Write using a **solution-oriented** tone and a **persuasive** writing style.

Formula

As a **[profession]** in the **[industry]**, could you provide a **[comprehensive strategy/thorough toolkit/detailed blueprint]** detailing the **[methods/techniques/approaches]** to identify what works well in **[my/our/their]** **[team/group/department]**'s interactions with **[clients/colleagues/stakeholders]**? Additionally, offer **[actionable steps/initial measures/immediate tactics]** for **[immediate/short-term/long-term]** implementation. Segment your insights into distinct modules, each supported by **[evidence from/references from/data from]** **[reputable journals/credible research/authoritative publications/industry reports]**. Investigate unexpected avenues and creative pathways. Let's **[examine each dimension meticulously/dissect this carefully]**. Write using a **[solution-oriented/pragmatic/analytical]** tone and a **[persuasive/engaging/innovative]** writing style.

Examples

Example 1: As a Customer Experience Specialist in the healthcare sector, could you provide a detailed blueprint outlining the techniques to identify what works well in my team's interactions with patients? Additionally, offer initial measures for short-term implementation. Segment your insights into distinct modules, each authenticated by corroborative evidence from credible sources. Explore unconventional approaches and diverse viewpoints. Let's examine each dimension meticulously. Write using a pragmatic tone and an engaging writing style.

Example 2: As a Business Relationship Manager in the automotive industry, could you provide a thorough toolkit outlining the approaches I can employ to identify what works well in my team's interactions with suppliers? Additionally, offer immediate tactics for long-term implementation. Segment your insights into distinct modules, each endorsed with data from verified academic publications. Unearth hidden gems and non-traditional methods. Let's dissect this carefully. Write using a solution-oriented tone and an innovative writing style.

PROMPT No 78

Tags

Authenticity - Presence - Interactions

Goal

To identify actionable strategies and techniques that enable team members to be fully present and authentic in their interactions with others. The aim is to enhance interpersonal relationships, foster a culture of trust, and ultimately improve team performance and well-being.

Prompt

As a **Behavioral Scientist** in the **pharmaceutical industry**, could you delineate a **multi-layered approach** to help **my team** be fully **present and authentic** in their interactions with **senior management**? Include **actionable strategies** that can be **immediately implemented**. Organize your insights into **distinct themes**, each supported by **references from reputable academic sources**. Delve into **unconventional solutions and alternative perspectives**. Let's examine each dimension meticulously. Write using an **inspiring** tone and an **engaging** writing style.

Formula

As a **[profession]** in the **[industry]**, could you delineate a **[multi-layered approach/comprehensive plan/structured methodology]** to help **[me/us/them]** be fully **[present/authentic/engaged]** in their interactions with **[others/clients/colleagues]**? Include **[actionable strategies/practical solutions/immediate steps]** for **[immediate/short-term/long-term]** implementation. Organize your insights into **[distinct themes/separate focal points/clear categories]**, each supported by **[references from/evidence from/data from]** **[reputable academic sources/credible research/authoritative publications]**. Delve into **[unconventional solutions/alternative perspectives/innovative methods]**. Let's **[examine each dimension meticulously/deconstruct this subject stepwise]**. Write using an **[inspiring/empowering/motivating]** tone and an **[engaging/invigorating/energetic]** writing style.

Examples

Example 1: As an Organizational Development Consultant in the automotive industry, could you delineate a comprehensive plan to help us ensure that our engineering team is fully present in their interactions with clients? Include practical solutions for immediate implementation. Organize your insights into separate focal points, each supported by evidence from credible research. Explore unconventional solutions and innovative methods. Let's deconstruct this subject stepwise. Write using an empowering tone and an invigorating writing style.

Example 2: As a Leadership Coach in the non-profit sector, could you delineate a structured methodology to help me ensure that my team is fully authentic in their interactions with colleagues? Include immediate steps for long-term implementation. Organize your insights into clear categories, each supported by data from authoritative publications. Probe into alternative perspectives and innovative methods. Let's examine each dimension meticulously. Write using a motivating tone and an energetic writing style.

PROMPT No 79

Triggers - Interactions - Compassionate

To identify and understand the triggers that typically cause team members to withdraw or shrink back during interactions, and to develop actionable strategies for mitigating these triggers. The focus is on creating a psychologically safe and inclusive environment that enhances team performance and well-being.

As an **Organizational Psychologist** in the **supply chain industry**, could you outline a **multi-faceted approach** to help **me** identify the triggers that typically cause **my** team to **withdraw or shrink back** in interactions? Include **actionable strategies** for **long-term** implementation. Organize your insights into **separate focal points**, each supported by **evidence from reputable journals**. Probe into **overlooked factors and innovative solutions**. Let's **scrutinize this topic incrementally**. Write using a **compassionate** tone and an **empathetic** writing style.

As a **[profession]** in the **[industry]**, could you outline a **[multi-faceted approach/comprehensive plan/structured methodology]** to help **[me/us/them]** identify the triggers that typically cause **[my/our/their]** team to **[withdraw/shrink back/disengage]** in interactions? Include **[actionable strategies/practical solutions/immediate steps]** for **[immediate/short-term/long-term]** implementation. Organize your insights into **[separate focal points/distinct themes/clear categories]**, each supported by **[evidence from/references from/data from]** **[reputable journals/credible research/authoritative publications]**. Probe into **[overlooked factors/innovative solutions/alternative perspectives]**. Let's **[scrutinize this topic incrementally/deconstruct this subject stepwise]**. Write using a **[compassionate/empathetic/supportive]** tone and an **[empathetic/understanding/considerate]** writing style.

Example 1: As a Team Dynamics Specialist in the healthcare industry, could you outline a comprehensive plan to help me identify the triggers that typically cause my nursing team to withdraw in interactions? Include practical solutions for short-term implementation. Organize your insights into distinct themes, each supported by references from credible research. Explore overlooked factors and innovative solutions. Let's deconstruct this subject stepwise. Write using a compassionate tone and an understanding writing style.

Example 2: As a Leadership Coach in the technology sector, could you outline a structured methodology to help us identify the triggers that typically cause our engineering team to disengage in interactions? Include immediate steps for long-term implementation. Organize your insights into clear categories, each supported by data from authoritative publications. Probe into alternative perspectives and innovative solutions. Let's scrutinize this topic incrementally. Write using an empathetic tone and a considerate writing style.

PROMPT No 80

Engagement - Strategy - Implementation

To obtain a comprehensive, actionable framework that outlines methods for specifying the ways in which others need to be involved in a project and strategies for inviting them to join. The aim is to enhance stakeholder engagement, improve project outcomes, and contribute to overall organizational success.

As a **Project Management Expert** in the **retail industry**, could you provide a **comprehensive strategy** detailing **methods** to specify the ways in which others need to be involved in **my** project and how to invite them to join? Additionally, offer **actionable steps** for **immediate** implementation. Segment your insights into distinct modules, each supported by **evidence from reputable industry reports**. Investigate unexpected avenues and creative pathways. Let's **examine each dimension meticulously**. Write using a **diplomatic** tone and a **persuasive** writing style.

As a **[profession]** in the **[industry]**, could you provide a **[comprehensive strategy/thorough toolkit/detailed blueprint]** detailing the **[methods/techniques/approaches]** to specify the ways in which others need to be involved in **[my/our/their]** project and how to invite them to join? Additionally, offer **[actionable steps/initial measures/immediate tactics]** for **[immediate/short-term/long-term]** implementation. Segment your insights into distinct modules, each supported by **[evidence from/references from/data from]** **[reputable journals/credible research/authoritative publications/industry reports]**. Investigate unexpected avenues and creative pathways. Let's **[examine each dimension meticulously/dissect this carefully]**. Write using a **[diplomatic/strategic/inviting]** tone and a **[persuasive/engaging/innovative]** writing style.

Example 1: As a Stakeholder Engagement Specialist in the automotive sector, could you provide a detailed blueprint outlining the techniques to specify the ways in which engineers and designers need to be involved in my project and how to invite them to join? Additionally, offer initial measures for short-term implementation. Segment your insights into distinct modules, each authenticated by corroborative evidence from credible sources. Explore unconventional approaches and diverse viewpoints. Let's dissect this carefully. Write using a strategic tone and an engaging writing style.

Example 2: As a Team Collaboration Advisor in the software industry, could you provide a thorough toolkit outlining the approaches I can employ to specify the ways in which developers and QA testers need to be involved in my project and how to invite them to join? Additionally, offer immediate tactics for long-term implementation. Segment your insights into distinct modules, each endorsed with data from verified academic publications. Unearth hidden gems and non-traditional methods. Let's examine each dimension meticulously. Write using a diplomatic tone and an innovative writing style.

PROMPT No 81

Dialogue - Professional - Unconventional

To furnish business leaders with a structured approach to initiate relationship enhancement with clients or colleagues, setting a foundation for improved communication and collaboration.

Act as a **Relationship Development Specialist** specializing in **Communication Skills** within the **corporate business sector**. Could you guide me through **a meticulous process to identify and execute the initial step in enhancing relationships with clients or colleagues**? Please include **analytical tools to assess the current state of relationships, communication strategies tailored for initiating relationship enhancement, and metrics to monitor the progress and effectiveness of the initiatives**. Ensure to cover how **to maintain a professional and constructive demeanor throughout this process**. Delve into innovative or unconventional solutions that could foster a culture of open dialogue and continuous relationship improvement. Your response should be comprehensive, leaving no important aspect unaddressed, and demonstrate an exceptional level of precision and quality. Let's think about this step by step. Write using a professional tone and a methodical writing style.

Act as a **[profession]** specializing in **[area of expertise]** within the **[industry]**. Could you guide me through **[specific challenge/opportunity]**? Please include **[methods/techniques]**. Ensure to cover how **[key areas/topics].** Delve into innovative or unconventional solutions that could foster a culture of open dialogue and continuous relationship improvement. Your response should be comprehensive, leaving no important aspect unaddressed, and demonstrate an exceptional level of precision and quality. Let's think about this step by step. Write using a **[type]** tone and a **[style]** writing style.

Example 1: Act as a Client Relationship Manager specializing in Emotional Intelligence within the financial sector. Could you guide me through a systematic approach to initiate the enhancement of relationships with key clients? Please include diagnostic frameworks for assessing relationship quality, communication techniques for expressing commitment to enhancement, and metrics for tracking relationship progress. Make sure to cover how to handle any resistance or hesitation from clients. Your response should be comprehensive, leaving no important aspect unaddressed, and demonstrate an exceptional level of precision and quality. Let's think about this step by step. Write using a solutions-oriented tone and a clear, instructional writing style.

Example 2: Act as a Team Building Consultant specializing in Conflict Resolution within the healthcare sector. Could you guide me through a structured approach for addressing concerns or issues raised by colleagues, as an initial step to improving inter-departmental relationships? Please include strategies for open dialogue, conflict resolution techniques, and mechanisms for ongoing feedback. Make sure to cover how to maintain a positive and constructive atmosphere during these discussions. Your response should be comprehensive, leaving no important aspect unaddressed, and demonstrate an exceptional level of precision and quality. Let's think about this step by step. Write using a balanced tone and a collaborative writing style.

PROMPT No 82

Tags

Resilience - Fulfillment - Problem-Solving

Goal

To obtain a comprehensive, actionable framework that outlines methods for identifying resources that can be accessed to face obstacles at work in a more fulfilled manner. The aim is to enhance personal resilience, improve problem-solving capabilities, and contribute to overall job satisfaction.

Prompt

As a **Professional Development Advisor** in the **education sector**, could you provide a **comprehensive action plan** detailing **methods** to identify resources **I** could access to face obstacles at work in a **more fulfilled manner**? Additionally, offer **actionable steps** for **immediate** implementation. Segment your insights into distinct modules, each supported by evidence from **reputable industry reports**. Investigate unexpected avenues and creative pathways. Let's **examine each dimension meticulously**. Write using a **solution-oriented** tone and a **persuasive** writing style.

Formula

As a [profession] in the [industry], could you provide a [comprehensive strategy/thorough action plan/detailed blueprint] detailing the [methods/techniques/approaches] to identify resources [I/we/they] could access to face obstacles at work in a [more fulfilled/more effective/more resilient] manner? Additionally, offer [actionable steps/initial measures/immediate tactics] for [immediate/short-term/long-term] implementation. Segment your insights into distinct modules, each supported by [evidence from/references from/data from] [reputable journals/credible research/authoritative publications/industry reports]. Investigate unexpected avenues and creative pathways. Let's [examine each dimension meticulously/dissect this carefully]. Write using a [solution-oriented/pragmatic/analytical] tone and a [persuasive/engaging/innovative] writing style.

Examples

Example 1: As a Career Coach in the finance sector, could you provide a detailed blueprint outlining the techniques to identify resources I could access to face obstacles at work in a more effective manner? Additionally, offer initial measures for short-term implementation. Segment your insights into distinct modules, each authenticated by corroborative evidence from credible sources. Explore unconventional approaches and diverse viewpoints. Let's dissect this carefully. Write using a pragmatic tone and an engaging writing style.

Example 2: As a Resilience Trainer in the manufacturing industry, could you provide a thorough toolkit outlining the approaches I can employ to identify resources to face obstacles at work in a more resilient manner? Additionally, offer immediate tactics for long-term implementation. Segment your insights into distinct modules, each endorsed with data from verified academic publications. Unearth hidden gems and non-traditional methods. Let's examine each dimension meticulously. Write using a solution-oriented tone and an innovative writing style.

PROMPT No 83

Habits - Cohesion - Frameworks

To identify and cultivate novel habits or behaviors that significantly bolster team performance and cohesion, and to delineate a structured approach for their development and integration within team dynamics.

Act as a **Team Development Specialist** specializing in **Habit Formation** within the **advertising industry**. Could you guide me through **a thorough exploration of new habits or behaviors that would notably enhance my team's performance and cohesion, and outline the methods for developing and integrating them**? Please include **frameworks for habit identification and assessment, strategies for habit cultivation, and tools for monitoring and reinforcing these new behaviors over time**. Ensure to cover how **to foster a supportive environment that encourages the adoption and sustained practice of these beneficial habits**. Delve into **innovative or unconventional approaches to habit formation that could further propel team effectiveness**. Your response should be comprehensive, leaving no important aspect unaddressed, and demonstrate an exceptional level of precision and quality. Let's think about this step by step. Write using a **motivational** tone and a **systematic, instructional** writing style.

Act as a **[profession]** specializing in **[area of expertise]** within the **[industry]**. Could you guide me through **[specific challenge/opportunity]**? Please include **[methods/techniques]**. Ensure to cover how **[key areas/topics]**. Delve into **[exploratory direction]** to **[desired outcome]**. Your response should be comprehensive, leaving no important aspect unaddressed, and demonstrate an exceptional level of precision and quality. Let's think about this step by step. Write using a **[type]** tone and a **[style]** writing style.

Example 1: Act as an Organizational Psychologist specializing in Behavior Change within the pharmaceutical industry. Could you guide me through the discovery and development of new habits or behaviors to significantly uplift my team's synergy and performance? Please include behavior assessment tools, habit formation strategies, and monitoring systems to gauge progress. Make sure to cover how to create a culture that values continuous improvement and supports the development of beneficial habits. Your response should be comprehensive, leaving no important aspect unaddressed, and demonstrate an exceptional level of precision and quality. Let's think about this step by step. Write using an analytical tone and a clear, instructional writing style.

Example 2: Act as a Performance Coach specializing in Positive Psychology within the hospitality industry. Could you guide me through a structured approach to identify and cultivate new habits or behaviors that will enhance my team's effectiveness and morale, and illustrate how to embed them within our daily operations? Please include positive reinforcement techniques, feedback loops, and tools for tracking behavioral changes over time. Make sure to cover how to build a supportive and encouraging environment for habit development. Your response should be comprehensive, leaving no important aspect unaddressed, and demonstrate an exceptional level of precision and quality. Let's think about this step by step. Write using an encouraging tone and a methodical writing style.

PROMPT No 84

Resilience - Introspection - Decision-making

To meticulously explore and understand the requisites for cultivating self-trust, and to establish a personalized plan that fosters a strong foundation of self-trust, thereby enhancing decision-making, resilience, and personal satisfaction.

Act as a **Self-Trust Facilitator** specializing in **Personal Resilience** within the **mental health industry**. Could you guide me through **a comprehensive exploration to discern what it entails for me to access self-trust optimally**? Please include **frameworks for self-reflection, strategies for building self-trust, and tools for monitoring and nurturing self-trust over time**. Ensure to cover how **to address and overcome barriers that may impede the development of self-trust**. Investigate pioneering or unconventional approaches that could fast-track the cultivation of self-trust. Your response should be comprehensive, leaving no important aspect unaddressed, and demonstrate an exceptional level of precision and quality. Let's think about this step by step. Write using an **introspective** tone and a **structured, instructional** writing style.

Act as a **[profession]** specializing in **[area of expertise]** within the **[industry]**. Could you guide me through **[specific challenge/opportunity]**? Please include **[methods/techniques]**. Ensure to cover how **[key areas/topics]**. Investigate pioneering or unconventional approaches that could fast-track the cultivation of self-trust. Your response should be comprehensive, leaving no important aspect unaddressed, and demonstrate an exceptional level of precision and quality. Let's think about this step by step. Write using a **[type]** tone and a **[style]** writing style.

Example 1: Act as a Confidence Coach specializing in Self-Efficacy within the coaching industry. Could you guide me through a profound journey to uncover what it takes for me to build and sustain self-trust? Please include self-assessment questionnaires, self-affirmation practices, and feedback mechanisms to track progress. Make sure to cover how to confront and surmount challenges that may hinder self-trust. Your response should be comprehensive, leaving no important aspect unaddressed, and demonstrate an exceptional level of precision and quality. Let's think about this step by step. Write using an encouraging tone and a clear, instructional writing style.

Example 2: Act as a Mindfulness Practitioner specializing in Inner Peace within the wellness industry. Could you guide me through an exploratory process to fathom the essentials for me to access self-trust in an optimal manner? Please include mindfulness exercises, emotional intelligence development, and tools for self-compassion and self-acceptance. Make sure to cover how to navigate through self-doubt and other potential barriers to self-trust. Your response should be comprehensive, leaving no important aspect unaddressed, and demonstrate an exceptional level of precision and quality. Let's think about this step by step. Write using a reflective tone and a step-by-step instructional writing style.

PROMPT No 85

Optimization - Assessment - Efficiency

To acquire a comprehensive, actionable guide on methods for optimally assessing the resources a company needs to better support the whole organization, with the aim of enhancing operational efficiency, employee satisfaction, and overall business performance.

As a **Resource Management Expert** in the **logistics industry**, could you provide an exhaustive guide outlining the methods I can employ to optimally assess the resources **my company** needs to better support the whole organization? Please include **both human capital and technological assets**. Organize your recommendations into thematic clusters, each supported by **data-driven evidence**. Explore unconventional approaches and diverse viewpoints. Let's dissect this carefully. Write using an **analytical** tone and a **structured** writing style.

As a **[profession]** in the **[industry]**, could you provide an exhaustive guide outlining the methods **[I/Name/Role]** can employ to optimally assess the resources **[my/our/their]** **[company/organization]** needs to better support the whole organization? Please include both **[human capital/technological assets]**. Organize your recommendations into thematic clusters, each supported by **[data-driven evidence/academic citations]**. Explore unconventional approaches and diverse viewpoints. Let's dissect this carefully. Write using a **[type]** tone and **[style]** writing style.

Example 1: As a Business Analyst in the healthcare industry, could you provide an exhaustive guide outlining the methods a hospital administrator can employ to optimally assess the resources needed to better support the entire hospital? Please include both medical staff and medical equipment. Break down your advice into specific sections, reinforcing each with quantifiable metrics and scholarly literature. Investigate unexpected avenues and creative pathways. Let's examine each dimension meticulously. Write using a focused tone and a concise writing style.

Example 2: As an Organizational Development Consultant in the software industry, could you provide an exhaustive guide outlining the methods I can employ to optimally assess the resources my tech company needs to better support the entire organization? Please include both engineering talent and software tools. Divide your insights into separate modules, each validated by empirical findings and authoritative sources. Unearth hidden gems and non-traditional methods. Let's tackle this in a phased manner. Write using a balanced tone and a nuanced writing style.

PROMPT No 86

Conflict - Communication - Legal

To acquire a comprehensive, actionable guide on best practices for speaking to a colleague about the factors that led him to have a fight with another colleague, with the aim of resolving the conflict, fostering a positive work environment, and maintaining team cohesion.

As a **Conflict Resolution Specialist** in the **legal industry**, could you provide an exhaustive guide outlining the best practices I should consider when speaking to a colleague about the factors that led **him** to have a fight with another colleague? Please include **both verbal communication strategies and non-verbal cues**. Structure your guidance into individual components, each backed by **statistical analysis and peer-reviewed studies**. Explore unconventional approaches and diverse viewpoints. Let's dissect this carefully. Write using an **analytical** tone and a **structured** writing style.

As a **[profession]** in the **[industry],** could you provide an exhaustive guide outlining the best practices **[I/Name/Role]** should consider when speaking to a colleague about the factors that led **[him/her/them]** to have a fight with another colleague? Please include both **[verbal communication strategies/non-verbal cues]**. Structure your guidance into individual components, each backed by **[statistical analysis/peer-reviewed studies]**. Explore unconventional approaches and diverse viewpoints. Let's dissect this carefully. Write using a **[type]** tone and **[style]** writing style.

Example 1: As an HR Consultant in the finance industry, could you provide an exhaustive guide outlining the best practices a team leader should consider when speaking to a financial analyst about the factors that led him to have a disagreement with another team member? Please include both active listening techniques and body language awareness. Divide your insights into separate modules, each validated by empirical findings and authoritative sources. Investigate unexpected avenues and creative pathways. Let's examine each dimension meticulously. Write using a focused tone and a concise writing style.

Example 2: As a Leadership Coach in the healthcare sector, could you provide an exhaustive guide outlining the best practices I should consider when speaking to a nurse about the factors that led her to have a conflict with another healthcare provider? Please include both empathetic questioning and appropriate eye contact. Break down your advice into specific sections, reinforcing each with quantifiable metrics and scholarly literature. Unearth hidden gems and non-traditional methods. Let's tackle this in a phased manner. Write using a balanced tone and a nuanced writing style.

PROMPT No 87

Talent - Assessment - Cohesion

To acquire a comprehensive, actionable guide on methods for identifying the unique qualities or attributes that make each team member stand out, particularly in alignment with the overall goals of the company. The aim is to foster individual growth, team cohesion, and organizational success.

Prompt

As a **Talent Management Specialist** in the **financial sector**, could you provide an exhaustive guide outlining the methods **my team** and I can employ to identify the unique qualities or attributes that make each team member stand out, considering **our company's overall goals**? Please include both **assessment tools and interpersonal evaluation techniques**. Segment the guide into **distinct categories**, and substantiate each with **empirical data and scholarly references**. Explore unconventional approaches and diverse viewpoints. Let's dissect this carefully. Write using an **analytical** tone and a **structured** writing style.

Formula

As a **[profession]** in the **[industry]**, could you provide an exhaustive guide outlining the methods **[I/Name/Role]** and **[my/our/their]** **[team/group/department]** can employ to identify the unique qualities or attributes that make each team member stand out, considering **[our/their]** company's overall goals? Please include both **[assessment tools/interpersonal evaluation techniques]**. Segment the guide into **[distinct categories]**, and substantiate each with **[empirical data/scholarly references]**. Explore unconventional approaches and diverse viewpoints. Let's dissect this carefully. Write using a **[type]** tone and **[style]** writing style.

Examples

Example 1: As a Human Resources Consultant in the healthcare industry, could you provide an exhaustive guide outlining the methods a department head can employ to identify the unique qualities or attributes that make each nurse stand out, considering the hospital's overall patient care goals? Please include both performance metrics and one-on-one interviews. Divide the guide into key areas, and validate each with clinical studies and peer-reviewed articles. Investigate unexpected avenues and creative pathways. Let's examine each dimension meticulously. Write using a focused tone and a concise writing style.

Example 2: As a Leadership Development Consultant in the manufacturing sector, could you provide an exhaustive guide outlining the methods I can employ to identify the unique qualities or attributes that make each assembly line worker stand out, considering the company's overall production goals? Please include both skill assessments and team feedback mechanisms. Break the guide into actionable steps, and corroborate each with industry benchmarks and case studies. Unearth hidden gems and non-traditional methods. Let's tackle this in a phased manner. Write using a balanced tone and a nuanced writing style.

PROMPT No 88

Tags

Self-awareness - Mindfulness - Growth

Goal

To meticulously develop and hone self-observance and self-awareness skills, fostering a deeper understanding of personal tendencies, behaviors, and responses, which in turn cultivates personal growth, enhanced interpersonal relations, and effective decision-making.

Prompt

Act as a **Self-Reflective Practices Expert** specializing in **Awareness Enhancement** within the **defense industry**. Could you guide me through **various strategies to significantly enhance my self-observance and self-awareness**? Please include **practical exercises, mindfulness techniques, and feedback mechanisms**. Ensure to cover how **to maintain a consistent practice of self-reflection and effectively utilize the insights gained for personal and professional development**. Explore **contemporary or avant-garde approaches** to **offer a fresh perspective on self-observance**. Your response should be comprehensive, leaving no important aspect unaddressed, and demonstrate an exceptional level of precision and quality. Let's think about this step by step. Write using an **introspective** tone and a **detailed, instructional** writing style.

Act as a **[profession]** specializing in **[area of expertise]** within the **[industry]**. Could you guide me through **[specific challenge/opportunity]**? Please include **[methods/techniques]**. Ensure to cover how **[key areas/topics]**. Explore **[exploratory direction]** to **[desired outcome]**. Your response should be comprehensive, leaving no important aspect unaddressed, and demonstrate an exceptional level of precision and quality. Let's think about this step by step. Write using a **[type]** tone and a **[style]** writing style.

Example 1: Act as a Mindfulness Coach specializing in Self-Observation Techniques within the wellness sector. Could you guide me through a series of strategies to improve my self-observance and self-awareness? Please include mindfulness exercises, reflective journaling, and feedback solicitation from peers. Make sure to cover how to integrate these practices into daily routines and leverage the insights for personal growth. Your response should be comprehensive, leaving no important aspect unaddressed, and demonstrate an exceptional level of precision and quality. Let's think about this step by step. Write using a nurturing tone and a clear, instructional writing style.

Example 2: Act as a Personal Insight Facilitator specializing in Awareness Expansion within the coaching industry. Could you guide me through diverse strategies to deepen my self-observance and self-awareness? Please include meditation practices, self-assessment tools, and constructive feedback mechanisms. Make sure to cover how to establish a supportive environment for continuous self-reflection and insight application. Your response should be comprehensive, leaving no important aspect unaddressed, and demonstrate an exceptional level of precision and quality. Let's think about this step by step. Write using an enlightening tone and a step-by-step instructional writing style.

SKILLS

PROMPT No 89

Skills - Gap - Analysis

To meticulously evaluate the discrepancy between the existing skills of the team and the requisite skills for attaining the organizational objectives, employing systematic methodologies which yield precise insights, enabling targeted development initiatives and optimal resource allocation in the technology consultancy sector.

As a **Skills Gap Analyst** specializing in **Corporate Performance Optimization** within the **technology consultancy sector**, how can I meticulously evaluate the discrepancy between my team's existing skills and the requisite skills for attaining our organizational objectives? Please provide a thorough elucidation of systematic methodologies encompassing **quantitative assessments, qualitative analyses, and feedback mechanisms**, aimed at yielding precise insights. The discourse should further delve into leveraging these insights for **targeted development initiatives, optimal resource allocation**, and **strategic planning to bridge the skills gap effectively**. Your discourse should be exhaustive, addressing all crucial aspects, and reflecting a high degree of precision and quality.

As a **[Profession]** specializing in **[Specialization]** within the **[Industry],** how can I meticulously evaluate the discrepancy between my team's existing skills and the requisite skills for attaining our organizational objectives? Please provide a thorough elucidation of systematic methodologies encompassing **[Assessment Techniques]**, aimed at yielding precise insights. The discourse should further delve into leveraging these insights for **[Development/Allocation Strategies]**, and **[Strategic Planning]** to bridge the skills gap effectively. Your discourse should be exhaustive, addressing all crucial aspects, and reflecting a high degree of precision and quality.

Example 1: As a Talent Development Strategist specializing in Organizational Excellence within the healthcare sector, how can I meticulously evaluate the discrepancy between my team's existing skills and the requisite skills for attaining our organizational objectives? Please provide a thorough elucidation of systematic methodologies encompassing competency assessments, behavioral analyses, and feedback loops, aimed at yielding precise insights. The discourse should further delve into leveraging these insights for targeted training programs, optimal resource allocation, and strategic planning to bridge the skills gap effectively. Your discourse should be exhaustive, addressing all crucial aspects, and reflecting a high degree of precision and quality.

Example 2: As a Performance Gap Auditor specializing in Corporate Skill Enhancement within the automotive sector, how can I meticulously evaluate the discrepancy between my team's existing skills and the requisite skills for attaining our organizational objectives? Please provide a thorough elucidation of systematic methodologies encompassing skills inventory, 360-degree feedback, and analytics, aimed at yielding precise insights. The discourse should further delve into leveraging these insights for personalized development plans, optimal resource allocation, and strategic planning to bridge the skills gap effectively. Your discourse should be exhaustive, addressing all crucial aspects, and reflecting a high degree of precision and quality.

PROMPT No 90

Skill - Leverage - Metrics

To acquire a comprehensive, actionable guide on methods for identifying the areas where a team has the highest leverage in terms of skill development, with the aim of maximizing team potential and aligning with organizational goals.

As a **Skill Development Analyst** in the **software industry**, could you provide an exhaustive guide outlining the methods **my team** and I can employ to identify the areas where we have the highest leverage in terms of **skill development**? Please include both **quantitative metrics and qualitative assessments**. Segment the guide into **distinct categories**, and substantiate each with **empirical data and scholarly references**. Explore unconventional approaches and diverse viewpoints. Let's dissect this carefully. Write using an **analytical** tone and a **structured** writing style.

As a **[profession]** in the **[industry]**, could you provide an exhaustive guide outlining the methods **[I/Name/Role]** and **[my/our/their]** **[team/group/department]** can employ to identify the areas where we have the highest leverage in terms of **[skill development/specific skills]?** Please include both **[quantitative metrics/qualitative assessments]**. Segment the guide into **[distinct categories],** and substantiate each with **[empirical data/scholarly references]**. Explore unconventional approaches and diverse viewpoints. Let's dissect this carefully. Write using a **[type]** tone and **[style]** writing style.

Example 1: As a Talent Development Consultant in the healthcare industry, could you provide an exhaustive guide outlining the methods a surgical team and their manager can employ to identify the areas where they have the highest leverage in terms of surgical skill development? Please include both performance evaluations and peer reviews. Divide the guide into key areas, and validate each with clinical studies and peer-reviewed articles. Investigate unexpected avenues and creative pathways. Let's examine each dimension meticulously. Write using a focused tone and a concise writing style.

Example 2: As a Leadership Development Consultant in the retail sector, could you provide an exhaustive guide outlining the methods my customer service team and I can employ to identify the areas where we have the highest leverage in terms of customer engagement skills? Please include both customer satisfaction scores and team self-assessments. Break the guide into actionable steps, and corroborate each with industry benchmarks and case studies. Unearth hidden gems and non-traditional methods. Let's tackle this in a phased manner. Write using a balanced tone and a nuanced writing style.

STRATEGIES

PROMPT No 91

Strategies - KPIs - Alignment

To proficiently formulate an array of effective strategies aimed at actualizing the key performance indicators (KPIs) of the team, ensuring a meticulous evaluation of each strategy for its potential impact and feasibility, within the context of strategic planning and execution.

As a **Strategic Performance Expert** specializing in **Outcome Optimization** within the **retail industry**, how can I proficiently devise a multitude of effective strategies targeted at actualizing my team's key performance indicators? I am seeking a thorough exposition on the methodological framework encompassing the generation, evaluation, and **iterative refinement** of strategies, infused with insights on **leveraging data analytics for informed decision-making**. The discourse should also articulate the importance of aligning these strategies with **organizational objectives**, while fostering a culture of **continuous improvement and adaptability** amidst **changing market dynamics**. Your elucidation should be comprehensive, addressing all critical aspects with a high degree of precision and quality.

As a **[Profession]** specializing in **[Specialization]** within the **[Industry]**, how can I proficiently devise a multitude of effective strategies targeted at actualizing my team's key performance indicators? I am seeking a thorough exposition on the methodological framework encompassing the generation, evaluation, and **[Iterative Aspect]** of strategies, infused with insights on **[Analytical/Technological Aspect for Informed Decision-making]**. The discourse should also articulate the importance of aligning these strategies with **[Organizational/Team Objective]**, while fostering a culture of **[Desired Cultural Aspect]** amidst **[Changing External Factor]**. Your elucidation should be comprehensive, addressing all critical aspects with a high degree of precision and quality.

Example 1: As a Performance Enhancement Specialist specializing in Tactical Execution within the automotive industry, how can I proficiently devise a multitude of effective strategies targeted at actualizing my team's key performance indicators? I am seeking a thorough exposition on the methodological framework encompassing the generation, evaluation, and adaptive refinement of strategies, infused with insights on leveraging predictive analytics for informed decision-making. The discourse should also articulate the importance of aligning these strategies with market penetration objectives, while fostering a culture of innovation and agility amidst evolving consumer preferences. Your elucidation should be comprehensive, addressing all critical aspects with a high degree of precision and quality.

Example 2: As an Operational Excellence Consultant specializing in Performance Metric Realization within the healthcare industry, how can I proficiently devise a multitude of effective strategies targeted at actualizing my team's key performance indicators? I am seeking a thorough exposition on the methodological framework encompassing the generation, evaluation, and continuous improvement of strategies, infused with insights on leveraging real-time data monitoring for informed decision-making. The discourse should also articulate the importance of aligning these strategies with patient satisfaction goals, while fostering a culture of quality assurance and compliance amidst changing regulatory landscapes. Your elucidation should be comprehensive, addressing all critical aspects with a high degree of precision and quality.

PROMPT No 92

Innovation - Realities - Resource

To equip business leaders with a robust framework for devising new strategies or plans that are not only innovative but also deeply aligned with the current situational realities, thereby ensuring practicality and effectiveness.

Act as a **Strategic Innovation Coach** specializing in the **healthcare industry**. Could you **guide** me through the **process** of **formulating** a **new strategy** that is **congruent** with the **current realities** of my **business environment**? Include **steps** for **situational analysis, stakeholder engagement, and resource allocation**. Let's methodically dissect each component. Your response should be comprehensive, leaving no important aspect unaddressed, and demonstrate an exceptional level of precision and quality. Write using a strategic tone and a prescriptive writing style.

Act as a **[profession]** specializing in the **[industry]**. Could you **[guide/lead/direct]** me through the **[process/framework/methodology]** of **[formulating/creating/developing]** a

[new/fresh/innovative] [strategy/plan/approach] that is
[congruent/aligned/synchronized] with the **[current/present/existing]**
[realities/situations/conditions] of my **[business/organization/team]**? Include
[steps/guidelines/measures] for **[situational analysis/stakeholder engagement/resource**
allocation]. Let's methodically dissect each component. Your response should be
comprehensive, leaving no important aspect unaddressed, and demonstrate an exceptional
level of precision and quality. Write using a **[type]** tone and **[style]** writing style.

Example 1: Act as a Business Transformation Specialist specializing in the logistics industry.
Could you lead me through the methodology of creating a new operational strategy that aligns
with the current market demands and supply chain complexities? Include guidelines for
market research, employee training, and technology integration. Let's sequentially address
each element. Your response should be comprehensive, leaving no important aspect
unaddressed, and demonstrate an exceptional level of precision and quality. Write using a
pragmatic tone and an actionable writing style.

Example 2: Act as a Leadership Development Coach specializing in the non-profit sector.
Could you guide me through the process of developing a new fundraising strategy that is
congruent with the current economic climate and donor behavior? Include steps for donor
segmentation, campaign design, and impact measurement. Let's tackle this in a phased
manner. Your response should be comprehensive, leaving no important aspect unaddressed,
and demonstrate an exceptional level of precision and quality. Write using an empathetic tone
and a consultative writing style.

STRENGTH

PROMPT No 93

Evolution - Passion - Self-assessment

To provide leaders with a comprehensive framework that enables their teams to
introspectively evaluate the evolution of their passion or joy for utilizing specific strengths over
time, thereby offering insights for personal and professional development.

Act as a **Career Development Consultant** specializing in the **financial services industry**.
Could you **delineate methods** for **my** team to **introspectively assess** whether their **passion**
or **joy** for using a **particular** strength has **increased or decreased** over the years? Include
self-assessment tools, key performance indicators, and reflective exercises. Let's
methodically dissect each component. Write using an introspective tone and a
research-based writing style. Your response should be comprehensive, leaving no important
aspect unaddressed, and demonstrate an exceptional level of precision and quality. Write
using an **empathetic** tone and a **community-focused** writing style.

Act as a **[profession]** specializing in the **[industry]**. Could you **[delineate/explain/outline]**
[methods/mechanisms/frameworks] for **[my/our/the]** team to
[introspectively/analytically/self-reflectively] [assess/evaluate/examine] whether their
[passion/joy/enthusiasm] for using a **[particular/specific/defined]** strength has
[increased/decreased/remained stable] over the **[years/months/period]**? Include
self-assessment tools, key performance indicators, and reflective exercises. Let's

methodically dissect each component. Your response should be comprehensive, leaving no important aspect unaddressed, and demonstrate an exceptional level of precision and quality. Write using a [type] tone and [style] writing style.

Example 1: Act as a Talent Development Specialist specializing in the automotive industry. Could you outline frameworks for my engineering team to analytically assess whether their enthusiasm for problem-solving has increased or decreased over the past five years? Include psychometric tests, project-based evaluations, and guided reflection sessions. Let's examine each dimension meticulously. Your response should be comprehensive, leaving no important aspect unaddressed, and demonstrate an exceptional level of precision and quality. Write using an analytical tone and a data-driven writing style.

Example 2: Act as a Leadership Coach specializing in the non-profit sector. Could you explain methods for my team to self-reflectively evaluate whether their passion for community outreach has increased or decreased over the past decade? Include journaling exercises, community impact metrics, and team discussions. Let's deconstruct this subject stepwise. Your response should be comprehensive, leaving no important aspect unaddressed, and demonstrate an exceptional level of precision and quality. Write using an empathetic tone and a community-focused writing style.

PROMPT No 94

Goal

Engagement - Strengths - Metrics

Tags

To provide leaders with a robust framework for engaging their teams in conversations that focus on identifying and discussing evidence of how individual strengths have manifested in their careers, thereby fostering self-awareness, career development, and team synergy.

Prompt

Act as a **Career Development Specialist** specializing in the **finance industry**. Could you elucidate a **comprehensive** set of **best practices** for **initiating and conducting** a **conversation** with my team about the **tangible** evidence they have of how their **strengths** have been **instrumental** in their **career trajectories**? Include **conversation starters, relevant theories, and metrics** for **gauging the effectiveness of the discussion**. Let's think about this step by step. Write using a **consultative** tone and an **advisory** writing style.

Formula

Act as a [profession] specializing in the [industry]. Could you elucidate a [comprehensive/robust/detailed] set of [best practices/guidelines/methodologies] for [initiating/conducting/facilitating] a [conversation/discussion/dialogue] with my team about the [tangible/concrete/observable] evidence they have of how their [strengths/skills/abilities] have been [instrumental/effective/critical] in their [career trajectories/career paths/professional journeys]? Include [conversation starters/question prompts/engagement techniques], [relevant theories/academic frameworks], and [metrics/KPIs/evaluation criteria] for [gauging/measuring/assessing] the [effectiveness/impact/success] of the [discussion/conversation/dialogue]. Let's think about this step by step. Write using a [type] tone and [style] writing style.

Example 1: Act as an HR Consultant specializing in the tech industry. Could you provide a robust set of guidelines for initiating a dialogue with my engineering team about the concrete evidence they have of how their problem-solving skills have positively impacted their career paths? Include question prompts, theories like Talent Management, and KPIs for measuring success. Let's piece-by-piece analyze this matter. Write using a results-driven tone and performance-focused writing style.

Example 2: Act as a Leadership Coach specializing in healthcare. Could you outline a detailed methodology for conducting a discussion with my nursing team about the observable evidence they have of how their empathetic skills have been critical in their professional journeys? Include engagement techniques, theories such as Emotional Intelligence, and evaluation criteria for gauging impact. Let's carefully evaluate each segment. Write using an empathetic tone and understanding writing style.

PROMPT No 95

Tags

Evaluation - Strengths - Allocation

Goal

To conduct a detailed evaluation of your team's unique strengths in order to identify tasks or activities that will not only come naturally to them but also optimize performance, job satisfaction, and overall team efficiency.

Prompt

As a **project manager** specializing in **digital transformation** within the **logistics industry**, provide an exhaustive and meticulous examination, incorporating innovative insights and inventive strategies for **pinpointing tasks or activities that will effortlessly align with your team's known strengths in analytical reasoning, adaptability, and collaboration**. Also, explore how to allocate these tasks for **maximized productivity**.

Formula

As a [profession] specializing in [area of expertise/focus] within the [industry], provide an exhaustive and meticulous examination, incorporating innovative insights and inventive strategies for [pinpointing tasks or activities that will effortlessly align with your team's known strengths in specific skill sets]. Also, explore how to allocate these tasks for [maximized productivity/well-being/efficiency].

Examples

Example 1: As a Sales Director specializing in enterprise software within the tech industry, provide an exhaustive and meticulous examination, incorporating innovative insights and inventive strategies, to identify the types of sales calls or client engagements that will come naturally to your team's strengths in relationship-building, negotiation, and technical knowledge. Also, explore the most effective ways to allocate these tasks for enhanced revenue generation.

Example 2: As an Academic Coordinator specializing in curriculum design within the higher education sector, provide an exhaustive and meticulous examination, incorporating innovative insights and inventive strategies, to discern which educational or administrative tasks will best match your team's strengths in instructional design, organizational skills, and student engagement. Also, explore optimal ways to delegate these tasks to improve educational outcomes.

PROMPT No 96

Understanding - Strengths - Engagement

To develop a deep, actionable understanding of how each team member's strengths manifest in their work and responsibilities, thereby enabling the leader to foster a workplace that amplifies these strengths for enhanced productivity and employee engagement.

As a **team leader** specializing in **Human Resources** within the **finance industry**, provide an exhaustive and meticulous examination, incorporating innovative insights and inventive strategies, for consciously identifying observable indicators or patterns that signify how each team member's strengths manifest in **tasks such as data analysis, customer interactions, and project management**. Further, share detailed guidance on how to disseminate these insights to secure buy-in from stakeholders.

As a **[profession]** specializing in **[area of expertise/focus]** within the **[industry]**, provide an exhaustive and meticulous examination, incorporating innovative insights and inventive strategies, for consciously identifying observable indicators or patterns that signify how each team member's strengths manifest in **[specific tasks or responsibilities]**. Further, share detailed guidance on how to disseminate these insights to secure buy-in from stakeholders.

Example 1: As a Marketing Manager specializing in digital advertising within the consumer goods industry, provide an exhaustive and meticulous examination, incorporating innovative insights and inventive strategies, for consciously identifying observable indicators or patterns that signify how each team member's strengths manifest in activities like campaign planning, SEO optimization, and consumer research. Further, share detailed guidance on how to disseminate these insights to secure buy-in from stakeholders.

Example 2: As a Principal Investigator specializing in biomedical research within the healthcare sector, provide an exhaustive and meticulous examination, incorporating innovative insights and inventive strategies, for consciously identifying observable indicators or patterns that signify how each research team member's strengths manifest in tasks such as data collection, analysis, and academic writing. Further, share detailed guidance on how to disseminate these insights to secure buy-in from stakeholders.

PROMPT No 97

Impacts - Strengths - Cohesion

To provide leaders with a comprehensive framework for evaluating the impacts of their individual strengths on interpersonal dynamics and team relationships, thereby enabling them to optimize their leadership style for enhanced team cohesion and performance.

As a **Leadership Development Consultant** specializing in the **finance industry**, could you **elucidate** the **impacts** that my **strengths** have on **others** and the **dynamics** of our **relationships**? Include **psychological theories, empirical evidence, and actionable**

strategies for **improvement**. Let's think about this step by step. Write using an **analytical** tone and a **data-driven** writing style.

As a **[profession]** specializing in the [industry], could you [elucidate/explain/clarify] the **[impacts/effects/consequences]** that my **[strengths/skills/abilities]** have on **[others/team members/colleagues]** and the **[dynamics/interactions/relations]** of our **[relationships/teamwork/collaboration]**? Include **[psychological theories/behavioral models]**, **[empirical evidence/research findings]**, and **[actionable strategies/practical steps]** for **[improvement/optimization/enhancement]**. Let's think about this step by step. Write using a **[type]** tone and **[style]** writing style.

Example 1: As an Organizational Psychologist specializing in the technology sector, could you explain the effects that my skills have on team members and the interactions of our teamwork? Include behavioral models, research findings, and practical steps for optimization. Let's systematically explore each facet. Write using a visionary tone and innovative writing style.

Example 2: As a Human Resources Advisor specializing in the manufacturing industry, could you clarify the consequences that my abilities have on colleagues and the dynamics of our collaboration? Include psychological theories, empirical evidence, and actionable strategies for enhancement. Let's carefully evaluate each segment. Write using a constructive tone and solution-focused writing style.

PROMPT No 98

Alignment - Competency - Realignment

To equip leaders, professionals, and team members with a comprehensive methodology for assessing the alignment between the requirements of a team's role or position and their actual strengths, thereby enabling targeted development and optimized performance.

Act as an **Organizational Psychologist** with a specialization in **talent alignment** in the **logistics industry**. Could you guide me through **a rigorous approach to assess the alignment between the requirements of my team's role and their actual strengths**? Please include **competency mapping, performance metrics, and psychological assessments**. Make sure to cover how **to interpret discrepancies and formulate action plans for realignment**. Investigate unconventional **talent management strategies** and cutting-edge **assessment tools** to **ensure accurate evaluations**. Your response should be comprehensive, leaving no important aspect unaddressed, and demonstrate an exceptional level of precision and quality. Let's think about this step by step. Write using an **analytical** tone and a **diagnostic** writing style.

Act as a **[profession]** with a specialization in **[area of expertise]** in the **[industry]**. Could you guide me through **[specific challenge/opportunity]**? Please include **[methods/techniques]**. Make sure to cover how **[key areas/topics]**. Investigate unconventional **[area for innovation]** and cutting-edge **[technologies/methods]** to **[desired outcome]**. Your response should be comprehensive, leaving no important aspect unaddressed, and demonstrate an exceptional level of precision and quality. Let's think about this step by step. Write using a **[type]** tone and **[style]** writing style.

Examples

Example 1: Act as a Talent Development Specialist with a specialization in skill assessment in the education sector. Could you guide me through a structured approach to assess the alignment between the requirements of my teaching staff's roles and their actual pedagogical strengths? Please include teaching evaluations, student feedback, and self-assessment tools. Make sure to cover how to address misalignments through targeted professional development. Explore the use of e-learning platforms and micro-credentialing to enhance skill alignment. Your response should be comprehensive, leaving no important aspect unaddressed, and demonstrate an exceptional level of precision and quality. Let's think about this step by step. Write using an instructional tone and a developmental plan style.

Example 2: Act as a Data Scientist with a specialization in workforce analytics in the retail industry. Could you guide me through a data-driven methodology to assess the alignment between the requirements of my sales team's roles and their actual selling strengths? Please include sales metrics, customer satisfaction surveys, and data visualization techniques. Make sure to cover how to recalibrate roles based on the findings and how to communicate these changes effectively. Delve into machine learning algorithms and predictive analytics to forecast future alignment scenarios. Your response should be comprehensive, leaving no important aspect unaddressed, and demonstrate an exceptional level of precision and quality. Let's think about this step by step. Write using an empirical tone and an analytical report style.

PROMPT No 99

Tags

Holistic - Fulfillment - Integration

Goal

To foster holistic development by guiding the team in consciously leveraging their inherent strengths across professional, personal, and community dimensions, enhancing fulfillment and well-being.

Prompt

As a **Leadership Development Specialist** specializing in **Strength-Based Development** within the **Management Consulting industry**, how can I meticulously devise and implement a holistic approach to encourage my team to consciously leverage their inherent strengths across all dimensions of their lives - professional, personal, and community engagements? I am seeking a thorough discussion elucidating actionable strategies, potential benefits, and the processes of integrating these strengths in a manner that significantly amplifies their sense of fulfillment and overall well-being. This discourse should encompass an insightful exploration of the ripple effects such an approach might have on individual performance, team synergy, and organizational culture, ensuring every crucial aspect is meticulously addressed with an exceptional degree of precision and quality.

Formula

As a **[Profession]** specializing in **[Specialization]** within the **[Industry],** how can I meticulously devise and implement a holistic approach to encourage my team to consciously leverage their inherent strengths across all dimensions of their lives - professional, personal, and community engagements? I am seeking a thorough discussion elucidating actionable strategies, potential benefits, and the processes of integrating these strengths in a manner that significantly amplifies their sense of fulfillment and overall well-being. This discourse should encompass an insightful exploration of the ripple effects such an approach might have on [individual performance/team synergy/organizational culture or other relevant impact areas], ensuring every crucial aspect is meticulously addressed with an exceptional degree of precision and quality.

Example 1: As a Fulfillment Strategy Analyst specializing in Strengths Utilization Frameworks within the Technology Sector, how can I meticulously devise and implement a holistic approach to encourage my team to consciously leverage their inherent strengths across all dimensions of their lives - professional, personal, and community engagements? I am seeking a thorough discussion elucidating actionable strategies, potential benefits, and the processes of integrating these strengths in a manner that significantly amplifies their sense of fulfillment and overall well-being. This discourse should encompass an insightful exploration of the ripple effects such an approach might have on project effectiveness, innovation culture, and client satisfaction, ensuring every crucial aspect is meticulously addressed with an exceptional degree of precision and quality.

Example 2: As an Empowerment Facilitator specializing in Holistic Strengths Application within the Education Sector, how can I meticulously devise and implement a holistic approach to encourage my team to consciously leverage their inherent strengths across all dimensions of their lives - professional, personal, and community engagements? I am seeking a thorough discussion elucidating actionable strategies, potential benefits, and the processes of integrating these strengths in a manner that significantly amplifies their sense of fulfillment and overall well-being. This discourse should encompass an insightful exploration of the ripple effects such an approach might have on teaching effectiveness, student engagement, and community outreach, ensuring every crucial aspect is meticulously addressed with an exceptional degree of precision and quality.

SUPPORT

PROMPT No 100

Support Structures - Needs Assessment - Alignment

To empower organizational leaders, professionals, and team managers with a comprehensive methodology for identifying the necessary structures or support mechanisms that the company should implement to enhance team performance, well-being, and overall effectiveness.

Act as an **Organizational Development Consultant** with a specialization in **team support structures** in the **pharmaceutical industry**. Could you guide me through **a comprehensive plan to identify what structures or support the company needs to implement to better support my team**? Please include **organizational design principles, employee engagement metrics, and resource allocation strategies**. Make sure to cover how **to conduct a needs assessment and how to align these structures with corporate objectives**. Investigate unconventional **support mechanisms** and cutting-edge **organizational theories** to **optimize team support**. Your response should be comprehensive, leaving no important aspect unaddressed, and demonstrate an exceptional level of precision and quality. Let's think about this step by step. Write using a **consultative** tone and a **strategic** planning style.

Act as a **[profession]** with a specialization in **[area of expertise]** in the **[industry]**. Could you guide me through **[specific challenge/opportunity]**? Please include **[methods/techniques]**. Make sure to cover how **[key areas/topics]**. Investigate unconventional **[area for innovation]** and cutting-edge **[technologies/methods]** to **[desired outcome]**. Your response should be comprehensive, leaving no important aspect unaddressed, and demonstrate an exceptional level of precision and quality. Let's think about this step by step. Write using a **[type]** tone and **[style]** writing style.

Example 1: Act as a Human Resources Strategist with a specialization in employee well-being in the hospitality industry. Could you guide me through a detailed plan to identify what structures or support the company needs to implement to better support my customer service team? Please include mental health initiatives, training programs, and work-life balance policies. Make sure to cover how to assess the current state of team well-being and how to measure the impact of new support structures. Explore the use of AI-driven HR analytics and employee feedback platforms to continuously adapt support mechanisms. Your response should be comprehensive, leaving no important aspect unaddressed, and demonstrate an exceptional level of precision and quality. Let's think about this step by step. Write using a compassionate tone and a well-being action plan style.

Example 2: Act as a Business Operations Specialist with a specialization in process optimization in the e-commerce industry. Could you guide me through a systematic approach to identify what structures or support the company needs to implement to better support my logistics team? Please include workflow automation tools, performance incentives, and cross-functional collaboration mechanisms. Make sure to cover how to evaluate the current operational bottlenecks and how to align new structures with growth objectives. Delve into lean methodologies and real-time tracking systems to enhance operational efficiency. Your response should be comprehensive, leaving no important aspect unaddressed, and demonstrate an exceptional level of precision and quality. Let's think about this step by step. Write using an operational tone and a process improvement style.

PROMPT No 101

Project Completion - Systems - Stakeholder Buy-in

To devise effective strategies and systems that will significantly aid the team in successfully completing specific projects and reaching targeted goals.

As a **project manager** specializing in **software development** within the **tech industry**, provide an exhaustive and meticulous examination, incorporating innovative insights and inventive strategies for **establishing** systems that will assist your team in **achieving particular** projects and goals. Explore how to **communicate** this plan and **secure** buy-in from **stakeholders**.

As a **[profession]** specializing in **[area of expertise/focus]** within the **[industry]**, provide an exhaustive and meticulous examination, incorporating innovative insights and inventive strategies for **[setting up/implementing/developing]** systems that will assist your team in **[achieving/completing/successfully finalizing]** **[particular/specific/targeted]** projects and goals. Explore how to **[communicate/share/impart]** this plan and **[secure/obtain/win]** buy-in from **[stakeholders/investors/team members]**.

Example 1: As a scrum master specializing in agile methodologies within the tech industry, provide an exhaustive and meticulous examination, incorporating innovative insights and inventive strategies for implementing systems that will help your development teams in successfully finalizing sprints and long-term goals. Explore how to share this plan and secure buy-in from team members.

Example 2: As a director of engineering specializing in operations within the manufacturing sector, provide an exhaustive and meticulous examination, incorporating innovative insights and inventive strategies for developing systems that will guide your teams in completing assembly line projects and operational objectives. Explore how to impart this plan and win buy-in from investors.

PROMPT No 102

Autonomy - Resources - Self-assessment

To empower your team to autonomously identify and articulate the resources, guidance, and support structures they require to confidently take the initial steps towards achieving specific goals or objectives.

As a **team leader** specializing in **product development** within the **tech industry**, provide an exhaustive and meticulous examination, incorporating innovative insights and inventive strategies, to design a **self-assessment framework** that enables your team to identify the types of **support, resources, or mentorship** they need to **initiate** their **goals** in the areas of **feature development, customer research, and scalability**. Also, explore how to disseminate this framework through different team layers and secure buy-in from stakeholders.

As a **[profession]** specializing in **[area of expertise/focus]** within the **[industry],** provide an exhaustive and meticulous examination, incorporating innovative insights and inventive strategies, to design a **[self-assessment framework/mechanism]** that enables your team to identify the types of **[support/resources/mentorship]** they need to **[initiate/embark on/begin]** their **[goals/objectives]** in the areas of **[specific project elements]**. Also, explore how to disseminate this framework through different team layers and secure buy-in from stakeholders.

Example 1: As an Operations Manager specializing in supply chain logistics within the automotive industry, provide an exhaustive and meticulous examination, incorporating innovative insights and inventive strategies, to develop a self-assessment tool that enables your team to identify the mentorship, tools, or training they need to begin optimizing inventory processes, supplier relationships, and production schedules. Also, explore how to disseminate this framework through different team layers and secure buy-in from stakeholders.

Example 2: As a Chief Nursing Officer specializing in patient care within the healthcare sector, provide an exhaustive and meticulous examination, incorporating innovative insights and inventive strategies, to establish a self-assessment questionnaire that helps your nursing team identify the kinds of support they require, be it additional staff, specialized training, or emotional well-being resources, to launch new initiatives in patient-centered care. Also, explore how to disseminate this framework through different team layers and secure buy-in from stakeholders.

VALUES

PROMPT No 103

Alignment - Engagement - Communication

To equip leaders, team members, and stakeholders in specific industries with a nuanced methodology for identifying and articulating shared values, thereby fostering alignment, engagement, and a cohesive organizational culture.

Act as a **Corporate Culture Strategist** with expertise in **value alignment** in the **insurance industry**. Could you guide me through **a systematic approach to identify and articulate the values of my organization that resonate with my own**? Please include **diagnostic surveys, stakeholder interviews, and data analysis techniques**. Make sure to cover how **to effectively communicate these shared values both internally and externally**. Explore unconventional avenues and innovative strategies **to deepen value alignment and engagement**. Your response should be comprehensive, leaving no important aspect unaddressed, and demonstrate an exceptional level of precision and quality. Let's think about this step by step. Write using an **insightful** tone and a **strategic** writing style.

Act as a **[profession]** with expertise in **[area of expertise]** in the **[industry]**. Could you guide me through **[specific challenge/opportunity]**? Please include **[methods/techniques]**. Make sure to cover how **[key areas/topics]**. Explore unconventional avenues and innovative strategies to **[desired outcome]**. Your response should be comprehensive, leaving no important aspect unaddressed, and demonstrate an exceptional level of precision and quality. Let's think about this step by step. Write using a [type] tone and [style] writing style.

Example 1: Act as an Organizational Development Consultant with expertise in employee engagement in the automotive industry. Could you guide me through a methodical approach to identify and express the values of my team that align with my personal values? Please include team workshops, value-mapping exercises, and feedback mechanisms. Make sure to cover how to integrate these values into team rituals and communication. Venture into the realm of behavioral economics and gamification to enhance value alignment. Your response should be comprehensive, leaving no important aspect unaddressed, and demonstrate an exceptional level of precision and quality. Let's think about this step by step. Write using an engaging tone and a how-to guide style.

Example 2: Act as a Business Ethicist with expertise in corporate responsibility in the pharmaceutical industry. Could you guide me through a rigorous process to identify and articulate the values of my company that align with societal needs? Please include stakeholder analysis, ethical frameworks, and impact assessments. Make sure to cover how to communicate these values to the public and potential investors. Delve into CSR strategies and ESG metrics to broaden the scope of value alignment. Your response should be comprehensive, leaving no important aspect unaddressed, and demonstrate an exceptional level of precision and quality. Let's think about this step by step. Write using a persuasive tone and an analytical writing style.

Tags

Reflection - Identification - Adaptation

Goal

To guide a team through a reflective and actionable process aimed at identifying and implementing changes to better align their actions and decisions with their core values, promoting authentic engagement and enhanced team synergy.

Prompt

Act as a **Team Values Alignment Strategist** with a specialization in **Reflective Practices** within the **healthcare industry**. Could you elucidate **a meticulous process to aid my team in introspecting and pinpointing adjustments for closer alignment with their core values**? Please encompass **structured reflection sessions, values identification exercises, and actionable adaptation strategies**. Ensure to elucidate on **fostering an environment conducive to open dialogue, employing feedback mechanisms for alignment validation, and gauging the ripple effects of the alterations on team coherence and output**. Venture into **pioneering methodologies to ensure sustained alignment amidst dynamic team landscapes**. Your response should be exhaustive, sparing no crucial detail, and epitomizing an exceptional caliber of precision and quality. Let's dissect this progressively. Write employing an **analytical** tone and a **methodical** writing style.

Formula

Act as a **[profession]** with a specialization in **[area of expertise]** within the **[industry]**. Could you elucidate **[specific challenge/opportunity]**? Please encompass **[methods/techniques]**. Ensure to elucidate on **[key areas/topics]**. Venture into **[additional exploration]**. Your response should be exhaustive, sparing no crucial detail, and epitomizing an exceptional caliber of precision and quality. Let's dissect this progressively. Write employing a **[type]** tone and a **[style]** writing style.

Examples

Example 1: Act as an Organizational Values Consultant with a specialization in Reflective Practices within the financial sector. Could you delineate a comprehensive process for aiding my team in reflection and identifying modifications for greater alignment with their intrinsic values? Please include reflective workshops, values mapping exercises, and change implementation blueprints. Ensure to delineate on establishing a culture of transparent communication, leveraging iterative feedback for alignment verification, and evaluating the broader ramifications of the modifications on team unity and efficacy. Delve into avant-garde techniques to maintain alignment amidst organizational evolution. Your response should be exhaustive, sparing no crucial detail, and epitomizing an exceptional caliber of precision and quality. Let's dissect this progressively. Write employing a reflective tone and a systematic writing style.

Example 2: Act as a Team Alignment Specialist with a specialization in Change Facilitation within the manufacturing sector. Could you unravel a detailed process to assist my team in introspection and pinpointing alterations to better align with their foundational values? Please encompass facilitated reflection sessions, values clarification exercises, and actionable change roadmaps. Ensure to unravel the tactics to create a conducive ambiance for candid discussions, utilizing continuous feedback for alignment assessment, and scrutinizing the extensive impact of the alterations on team harmony and productivity. Explore cutting-edge methodologies to foster sustained alignment amidst shifting team dynamics. Your response should be exhaustive, sparing no crucial detail, and epitomizing an exceptional caliber of precision and quality. Let's dissect this progressively. Write employing an insightful tone and a structured writing style.

PROMPT No 105

Workshops - Dialogue - Methodologies

To develop a collaborative approach for engaging the team in exploring the utilization of shared values as a guiding framework to foster informed and congruent decision-making that aligns with organizational objectives.

Act as a **Values Integration Consultant** with a specialization in **Decision-Making Frameworks** within the **healthcare industry**. Could you guide me through **a collaborative process to engage my team in exploring how we can utilize our shared values as a guiding framework to make better choices**? Please include **interactive workshops, reflection sessions, and real-world scenario simulations**. Make sure to cover how **to foster open dialogue, ensure the alignment of individual and organizational values, and measure the impact of value-guided decision-making on team cohesion and organizational effectiveness**. Delve into **pioneering methodologies to ensure a deep-rooted understanding and consistent application of these values in our decision-making processes**. Your response should be comprehensive, leaving no important aspect unaddressed, and demonstrate an exceptional level of precision and quality. Let's think about this step by step. Write using a **collaborative** tone and a **solution-oriented** writing style.

Act as a **[profession]** with a specialization in **[area of expertise]** within the **[industry]**. Could you guide me through **[specific challenge/opportunity]**? Please include **[methods/techniques]**. Make sure to cover how **[key areas/topics]**. Delve into **[additional exploration]**. Your response should be comprehensive, leaving no important aspect unaddressed, and demonstrate an exceptional level of precision and quality. Let's think about this step by step. Write using a **[type]** tone and a **[style]** writing style.

Example 1: Act as an Ethical Leadership Advisor with a specialization in Value-Driven Decision Making within the non-profit sector. Could you guide me through a team-engagement process to delve into how our shared values can serve as a guiding compass for making better choices? Please include ethical discussions, value-alignment workshops, and practical scenario-based exercises. Make sure to cover how to create a safe space for open discussions, align personal values with organizational values, and evaluate the effectiveness of value-based decisions in enhancing team collaboration and advancing organizational goals. Explore groundbreaking methodologies to ensure the ingrained understanding and application of these values in our day-to-day decisions. Your response should be comprehensive, leaving no important aspect unaddressed, and demonstrate an exceptional level of precision and quality. Let's think about this step by step. Write using an engaging tone and an action-driven writing style.

Example 2: Act as a Corporate Values Strategist with a specialization in Team Decision-Making within the technology sector. Could you guide me through a participatory approach to engage my team in exploring how our collective values can be harnessed as a guiding framework for enriched decision-making? Please include facilitated dialogue sessions, value-mapping exercises, and feedback mechanisms. Make sure to cover how to encourage value articulation, ensure the congruence of team decisions with organizational ethos, and gauge the impact of value-aligned choices on team dynamics and organizational performance. Venture into innovative approaches to ensure a sustained commitment to value-driven decision-making. Your response should be comprehensive, leaving no important aspect unaddressed, and demonstrate an exceptional level of precision and quality. Let's think about this step by step. Write using a constructive tone and a forward-thinking writing style.

PROMPT No 106

BestPractices - Values - TeamCohesion

To provide leaders and team members with a nuanced understanding of best practices when discussing the identification of small, actionable steps to live more consistently with their values. The objective is to foster a values-driven culture, improve team cohesion, and enhance individual and collective performance.

As an **Organizational Psychologist** in the **technology sector**, could you delineate **best practices** I should consider when **engaging in conversations** with **my** team about identifying **one** small step they can take to live more consistently with their **values**? Include **actionable recommendations** and **real-world examples**. Organize your insights into **thematic clusters**, each supported by evidence from **reputable industry reports**. Explore **unconventional solutions and alternative perspectives**. Let's **deconstruct this subject stepwise**. Write using a **consultative** tone and an **advisory** writing style.

As a **[profession]** in the **[industry]**, could you delineate **[best practices/guidelines/recommendations]** I should consider when **[engaging in conversations/chatting]** with **[my/our]** team about identifying **[one/a]** small step they can take to live more consistently with their **[values/principles]**? Include **[actionable recommendations/practical advice/feasible solutions]** and **[real-world examples/case studies]**. Organize your insights into **[thematic clusters/distinct categories]**, each supported by **[evidence from/references from/data from]** **[reputable industry reports/credible research/authoritative publications]**. Explore **[unconventional solutions/creative pathways/alternative perspectives]**. Let's **[deconstruct this subject stepwise/examine this topic in detail]**. Write using a **[consultative/engaging]** tone and an **[advisory/informative]** writing style.

Example 1: As a Team Development Specialist in the healthcare industry, could you delineate guidelines I should consider when chatting with my team about identifying one small step they can take to live more consistently with their principles? Include practical advice and case studies. Organize your insights into distinct categories, each supported by references from credible research. Explore unconventional solutions and creative pathways. Let's examine this topic in detail. Write using an engaging tone and an informative writing style.

Example 2: As a Leadership Coach in the education sector, could you delineate best practices I should consider when engaging in conversations with my team about identifying a small step they can take to live more consistently with their values? Include feasible solutions and real-world examples. Organize your insights into thematic clusters, each supported by evidence from authoritative publications. Explore alternative perspectives and creative pathways. Let's deconstruct this subject stepwise. Write using a consultative tone and an advisory writing style.

PROMPT No 107

Tags

Relationships - Cohesion - Productivity

Goal

To obtain a comprehensive, actionable framework that identifies the core values essential for creating and maintaining meaningful and productive relationships within a team, as well as actionable steps to live those values more fully. The aim is to foster team cohesion, improve interpersonal relationships, and enhance overall productivity.

Prompt

As a **Team Cohesion Specialist** in the **television industry**, could you provide a **comprehensive strategy** detailing the **core values** that can guide **my team** in creating and maintaining meaningful and productive relationships with **others**? Additionally, offer **actionable steps** for living these values more fully. Divide your recommendations into distinct areas, each supported by **evidence from sources**. Investigate unexpected avenues and creative pathways. Let's dissect this carefully step by step. Write using a **visionary** tone and an **innovative** writing style.

Formula

As a **[profession]** in the **[industry]**, could you provide a **[comprehensive strategy/thorough toolkit/detailed blueprint]** detailing the **[core values/principles/ethics]** that can guide **[my/our/their] [team/group/department]** in creating and maintaining meaningful and productive relationships with **[others/clients/stakeholders]**? Additionally, offer **[actionable steps/initial measures/immediate tactics]** for living these values more fully. Divide your recommendations into distinct areas, each supported by **[evidence from/references from/data from] [reputable sources/credible research/authoritative publications]**. Investigate unexpected avenues and creative pathways. Let's dissect this carefully step by step. Write using a **[visionary/inspirational/consultative]** tone and an **[innovative/nuanced/engaging]** writing style.

Examples

Example 1: As an Organizational Culture Consultant in the technology sector, could you provide a detailed blueprint outlining the core values that can guide a software development team in creating and maintaining meaningful and productive relationships with clients? Additionally, offer initial measures for living these values more fully. Divide your recommendations into distinct areas, each authenticated by corroborative evidence from credible sources. Explore unconventional approaches and diverse viewpoints. Let's examine each dimension meticulously. Write using an inspirational tone and an engaging writing style.

Example 2: As a Leadership Development Coach in the education sector, could you provide a thorough toolkit outlining the principles that can guide a faculty team in creating and maintaining meaningful and productive relationships with students? Additionally, offer immediate tactics for living these principles more fully. Divide your recommendations into distinct areas, each endorsed with data from verified academic publications. Unearth hidden gems and non-traditional methods. Let's dissect this carefully. Write using a visionary tone and an innovative writing style.

WEAKNESS

PROMPT No 108

Tags

Strengths - Optimization - Productivity

Goal

To gain specific methodologies or tactics that can be implemented to accurately evaluate and leverage the individual strengths and weaknesses of team members, with the goal of optimizing their capabilities and improving overall team productivity.

Prompt

As a **Team Development Specialist**, adopting a **solution-oriented and constructive tone**, could you provide specific methodologies or tactics that can be implemented to **accurately evaluate and leverage the individual strengths and weaknesses** of **my team members**? This is particularly relevant given the goal of **optimizing their capabilities and improving overall team productivity**.

Formula

As a **[profession]**, adopting a **[tone of voice]**, could you provide specific methodologies or tactics that can be implemented to **[contextual challenge/opportunity]** of **[my/their]** **[team/group/department]**? This is particularly relevant given the goal of **[desired outcome]**.

Examples

Example 1: As a Human Resources Consultant, adopting a supportive and empathetic tone, could you provide specific methodologies or tactics that can be implemented to accurately evaluate and leverage the individual strengths and weaknesses of my sales team? This is particularly relevant given the goal of optimizing their capabilities and improving overall sales performance.

Example 2: Adopting a motivational and encouraging tone, as a Leadership Development Consultant, could you provide specific methodologies or tactics that can be implemented to accurately evaluate and leverage the individual strengths and weaknesses of their faculty? This is particularly relevant given the goal of optimizing their capabilities and improving overall academic performance.

PROMPT No 109

Tags

Team-Weaknesses - Negative-Outcomes - Strategies

Goal

To gain a comprehensive understanding of potential negative outcomes that may arise from team's weaknesses at work and to effectively address them using specific strategies, methods, or approaches.

Prompt

As a **Team Development Specialist**, adopting a **solution-oriented and analytical tone**, could you suggest specific strategies, methods, or approaches that I can use to **effectively explore and uncover any potential negative outcomes** that may arise from **our team's** weaknesses at work? This is particularly relevant given the goal of **gaining a comprehensive understanding and effectively addressing these issues**.

Formula

As a **[profession]**, adopting a **[tone of voice]**, could you suggest specific strategies, methods, or approaches that **[I/Name/Role]** can use to **[contextual challenge/opportunity]** that may arise from **[my/their]** **[team/group/department]**'s weaknesses at work? This is particularly relevant given the goal of **[desired outcome]**.

Examples

Example 1: As a Human Resources Consultant, adopting a proactive and analytical tone, could you suggest specific strategies, methods, or approaches that a department head can use to effectively explore and uncover any potential negative outcomes that may arise from their faculty's weaknesses at work? This is particularly relevant given the goal of gaining a comprehensive understanding and effectively addressing these issues.

Example 2: As a Leadership Coach, adopting a solution-oriented and analytical tone, could you suggest specific strategies, methods, or approaches that I can use to effectively explore and uncover any potential negative outcomes that may arise from my sales team's weaknesses at work? This is particularly relevant given the goal of gaining a comprehensive understanding and effectively addressing these issues.

ROMPT No 110

Tags

Reflection - Artificial-Intelligence - Weaknesses

Goal

To create an effective strategy for business leaders to initiate and facilitate an impactful discussion with their teams on identifying weaknesses at work. The conversation aims to encourage self-awareness, constructive feedback, and actionable plans for improvement. This will ultimately lead to increased productivity, team cohesion, and personal and professional growth.

Prompt

As a **Leadership Development Coach** with a specialization in **team effectiveness** for the **artificial intelligence and machine learning industry**. Could you guide me through the **process of holding a thoughtful discussion with my team to explore their weaknesses at work**? Please include **methods for initiating the conversation, the types of questions to ask, techniques for fostering an environment where team members feel safe sharing,**

and follow-up steps for creating actionable improvement plans. Ensure that the guide covers **how to encourage self-assessment, peer-to-peer feedback, and how to turn weaknesses into areas for growth**. Introduce unique angles and prophetic opportunities. Let's think about this step by step. Write using an **informative** tone and **factual** writing style.

As a [profession] with specialization in [topic/specialization] for the [industry]. Could you guide me through the [contextual challenge/opportunity]? Please include [methods//techniques/steps]. Ensure that the guide covers [aspects/topics]. Introduce unique angles and prophetic opportunities. Let's think about this step by step. Write using a [type] tone and [style] writing style.

Example 1: As a Business Strategy Consultant with a focus on Team Productivity for the insurance industry, could you guide me through the method for initiating a proactive dialogue with my team to explore the weaknesses they might be facing in workflow efficiency? Include icebreakers for initiating the conversation, questions that encourage honest feedback, techniques for creating a non-judgmental space, and strategies for post-conversation action planning. Make sure the guide includes elements of self-assessment tools like the Eisenhower Matrix and methods for peer review. Advocate for disruptive strategies and unorthodox viewpoints. Let's analyze this piece by piece. Write using a friendly tone and approachable writing style.

Example 2: As a Professional Development Coach with a focus on Emotional Intelligence, could you walk me through the strategy for holding an open discussion with my team to identify weaknesses in interpersonal skills? Incorporate techniques for kicking off the conversation, types of questions that foster self-reflection, approaches to ensure psychological safety, and next steps to facilitate individual growth plans. Ensure the guide elaborates on how to employ emotional intelligence assessments and peer feedback for holistic understanding. Illuminate obscure techniques and transformative solutions. Let's dissect this carefully. Write using an analytical tone and systematic writing style.

PROMPT No 111

Improvement - HR - Competencies

To gain specific strategies for accurately assessing areas of improvement or skill acquisition for a team, and to learn about an actionable plan for helping the team acquire or develop these skills, thereby enhancing their overall abilities.

As a **Human Resources Consultant**, adopting a **solution-oriented tone**, could you provide specific strategies that I can use to accurately assess the areas in which **my team** needs to **improve or acquire skills and competencies**? Furthermore, could you suggest a specific steps or action plan that can be implemented to aid them in **acquiring or developing these identified skills or competencies**, thereby enhancing their overall abilities?

As a [profession], adopting a [tone of voice], could you provide specific strategies that [I/Name/Role] can use to accurately assess the areas in which [my/their] [team/group/department] needs to [contextual challenge/opportunity]? Furthermore, could you suggest a specific steps or action plan that can be implemented to aid them in **[desired outcome]**, thereby enhancing their overall abilities?

Example 1: As a Leadership Development Consultant, adopting a proactive and constructive tone, could you provide specific strategies that a department head can use to accurately assess the areas in which their faculty needs to improve or acquire academic competencies? Furthermore, could you suggest a specific steps or action plan that can be implemented to aid them in acquiring or developing these identified skills or competencies, thereby enhancing their overall academic abilities?

Example 2: As a Team Coach, adopting an encouraging and supportive tone, could you provide specific strategies that I can use to accurately assess the areas in which my project team needs to improve or acquire project management skills? Furthermore, could you suggest a specific steps or action plan that can be implemented to aid them in acquiring or developing these identified skills or competencies, thereby enhancing their overall project management abilities?

Final Words

In the domain of coaching, mentoring, and leadership, navigating the complexities requires a disciplined approach. This book aims to be an instrumental guide, leveraging artificial intelligence and prompt engineering to provide actionable insights for those in any profession. I have presented a curated list of prompts, each serving a specific objective: to clarify roles, define leadership strategies, and optimize coaching techniques, to name a few.

The scope of this book goes beyond a mere compilation of prompts. My goal is to impart a strategic mindset for interpreting challenges as opportunities, seeing barriers as milestones for growth, and viewing the future as a dynamic environment that can be strategically managed.

For the reader who began with skepticism, I hope you conclude this book with a newfound confidence, equipped with a toolkit that elevates your professional standing. For the experienced practitioner, may the methods and strategies here serve to refine your existing approaches.

This journey, while individual in nature, is set against the backdrop of collective human experience. Artificial intelligence serves as a bridge to this collective wisdom, streamlining the path toward your professional and personal development objectives.

In summary, this book aims to leave you not just prepared but empowered. As you close this chapter and move forward in your career, be reminded that each decision and action point offers an opportunity for growth and leadership. This is not just preparation; it is empowerment for transformative impact.

The challenges you face should be viewed as opportunities for demonstrating your leadership and expertise. I encourage you to approach these with a strategic focus, grounded in the knowledge and insights you have gained from this book.

I wish you all the best.

Mauricio

P.S. To leave your review, please scan this QR code:

APPENDIXES

Appendix No 1

Sign-In to Chatbots

1,1. Chat GPT

Step 1: Visit ChatGPT on https://chat.openai.com/chat Click on "Sign Up" and then create your account.

Step 2: Verify your Account. You'd have to enter your details, verify your email and give an OTP you'll receive on your phone.

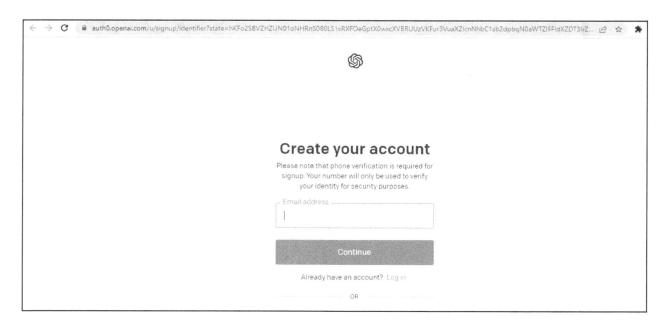

Once done, you'd have access to the free version of ChatGPT

As of April 2023, ChatGPT 3.5 is free to use and ChatGPT-4 costs $20 per month. As a beginner, you can easily test your skills on the free version.

This is how it looks:

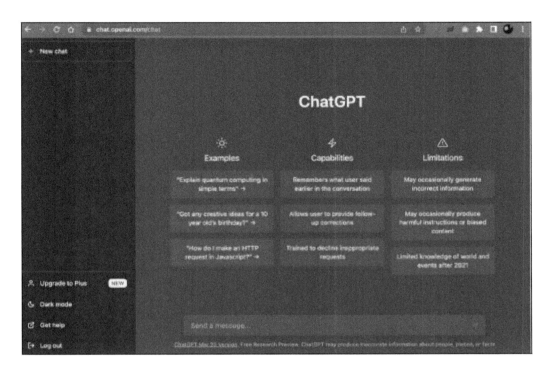

At the very bottom is where you'd chat:

You can now ask GPT anything you want, and it'll give you the desired result

Note: The procedure outlined was developed based on the instructions available at the time of writing. If you require further assistance with signing up for ChatGPT, please scan this QR code:

1.2. Bing Chat

Step 1: Go to the Microsoft website (www.microsoft.com).

Locate the download page for Edge or look for "Microsoft Edge" in the search bar. If you don't want to download Microsoft Edge, go directly to Step 6. For better results, we recommend using Microsoft Edge.

Step 2: Click the download button and choose the version that fits your system.

Step 3: Once downloaded, open the setup file.

Step 4: A User Account Control dialog box will appear – click "Yes" to grant permission.

The installation wizard will guide you through a series of prompts and options. Review them carefully.

Step 5: To open Microsfot Edge, press Win + R on the keyboard to open the Run window. In the Open field, type "microsoft-edge:" and press Enter on the keyboard or click or tap OK. Microsoft Edge is now open.

Step 6: Head to bing.com/chat

Step 7: From the pop-up that appears, click 'Start chatting'

Step 8: Enter the email address for the Microsoft account you'd like to use and click 'Next'.

If you don't have one, click 'Create one!' just under the text box and follow the instructions. Enter your password when prompted and click Next. From the following screen, choose whether you'd like to stay signed in or not. Click 'Chat Now'

Step 9: Choose your conversation style. If you've never used it before, it's best to stick with 'More Balanced'

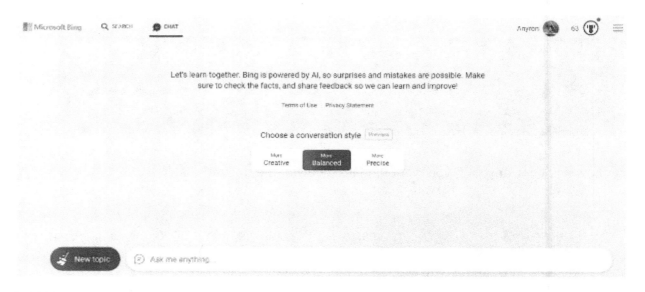

That's it! You can now start chatting.

A possible 3-course menu for 6 people who don't like nuts or seafood is:

- **Starter:** Vegetable soup with gluten-free bread. Warm and healthy dish with various veggies and herbs.
- **Main:** Roasted chicken with roasted potatoes and green beans. Classic and satisfying dish with garlic, lemon, and rosemary.

Welcome to the new Bing, your AI-powered co-pilot for the web.

Note: The procedure outlined was developed based on the instructions available at the time of writing. If you require assistance with signing up for Bing Chat, please scan this QR code:

1.3. Google Bard

Step 1: Go to bard.google.com. Select Try Bard. Accept Google Bard Terms of Service

Step 2: Go to "Sign in"

Step 3: Enter a query or search term and then hit enter.

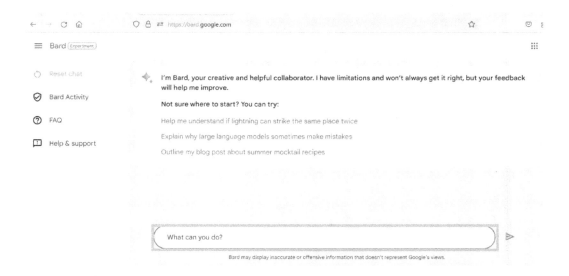

Wait for the AI to respond. You can then either continue the conversation or select Google It to use the traditional search engine.

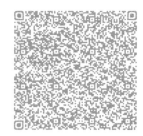

Note: The procedure outlined was developed based on the instructions available at the time of writing. If you require assistance with signing up for Google Bard, please scan this QR code:

1.4. Meta LLaMA

Getting the Models

Step 1: Go to https://ai.meta.com/resources/models-and-libraries/llama-downloads/

Step 2: Fill the form with your information.

Step 3: Accept their license (if you agree with it)

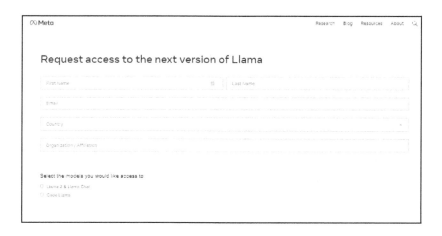

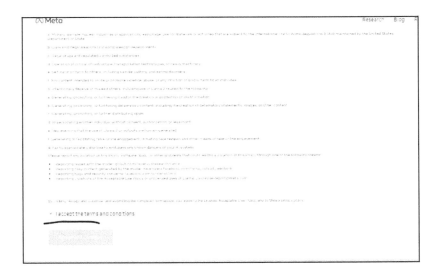

Step 4: Once your request is approved, you will receive a signed URL over email.

Step 5: Clone the Llama 2 repository (go to https://github.com/facebockresearch/llama).

Step 6: Run the download.sh script, passing the URL provided when prompted to start the download. Keep in mind that the links expire after 24 hours and a certain amount of downloads. If you start seeing errors such as 403: Forbidden, you can always re-request a link.

Appendix No 2

Follow-up Prompts

There are 1100 prompts that you can use as follow-ups in order to get more specific or revised information from ChatGPT and other Chatbots. Don't forget to tailor these prompts to your specific circumstances and to the response you previously received from the Chatbot.

Each of these prompt types serves a different purpose and can be used effectively in different scenarios. Depending on the context and the intended outcome, one type of prompt may be more suitable than another.

These prompts are divided into eleven distinct categories, each tailored to specific conversational needs: Generic, Enhancement, Clarification, Probing, Critical Thinking, Instructional, Exploration, Comparison, Summarization, Evaluation, and Hypothetical.

To have access to 1100 follow-up prompts, please scan this QR code:

Appendix No 3

A Beginner's Step-by-Step Guide to Using ChatGPT

If you're new to ChatGPT, don't fret. This guide is designed to walk you through its use, step by step. By the end, you'll have a solid grasp of how to harness the power of this incredible tool.

Step 1: Accessing the Platform

Visit OpenAI's Platform: Head to OpenAI's official website: ChatGPT [openai.com]

Sign Up/Log In: If you don't have an account, you'll need to sign up. If you already have one, simply log in.

Step 2: Navigating the Interface

Dashboard: This is your central hub, where you can access various tools and see your usage stats.

Start a New Session: To interact with ChatGPT, start a new session or use a predefined platform depending on the current interface.

Step 3: Interacting with ChatGPT

Input Field: This is where you'll type or paste the prompts from our book.

Submit: Once you've entered your prompt, press 'Enter' or click the 'Submit' button.

Review Output: ChatGPT will generate a response. Take a moment to read and understand it.

Step 4: Refining Your Interaction

Being Specific: If you need specific information or a particular type of response, make your prompts more detailed.

Iterate: If the first response isn't what you're looking for, tweak your prompt and try again.

Step 5: Utilizing the Prompts from This Book

Choose a Prompt: Browse the book's prompt section and select one that aligns with your current needs.

Input: Copy and paste or type the chosen prompt into ChatGPT's input field.

Customization: Feel free to adjust the prompts to be more specific to your situation.

Step 6: Safety and Best Practices

Sensitive Information: Never share sensitive personal information, such as Social Security numbers or bank details, with ChatGPT or any online platform.

Understanding Outputs: Remember, while ChatGPT can produce human-like responses, it doesn't understand context in the same way humans do. Always review its advice with a critical eye.

Step 7: Exploring Advanced Features

As you become more comfortable with ChatGPT:

Experiment: Play around with different types of prompts to see the diverse responses you can get.

Integrate with Other Tools: There are several third-party tools and platforms that have integrated ChatGPT. Explore these to maximize your work.

Step 8: Stay Updated

Technology, especially in the AI field, evolves rapidly. Periodically check OpenAI's official channels for updates, new features, or changes to the platform.

By following this guide, even the most tech-averse individuals will find themselves comfortably navigating and interacting with ChatGPT. As we delve deeper into the book and introduce specific prompts tailored for your work you'll be equipped with the knowledge to make the most of them.

Here is our "*Elevate Your Productivity Using ChatGPT*" Guide: To access this guide to boost your efficiency and productivity, please scan this QR code.

Appendix No 4

Mentoring, Coaching, and Leadership Professionals

This list encompasses professions pivotal in nurturing growth, leadership, and collaboration in work settings. They play crucial roles in guiding, training, and inspiring individuals towards achieving personal and organizational objectives.

1. Mentor: Provides guidance, support, and wisdom to less experienced individuals for personal and professional growth.
2. Coach: Assists in developing specific skills, improving performance, and achieving defined objectives through structured guidance.
3. Leader: Guides, inspires, and influences a group towards achieving common goals, fostering positive organizational culture.
4. Executive Coach: Assists executives in honing leadership skills, achieving goals, and navigating career transitions.
5. Life Coach: Guides individuals in personal development, goal-setting, and achieving life balance.
6. Career Counselor: Provides advice on career exploration, development strategies, and job search.
7. Organizational Consultant: Aids organizations in improving performance, culture, and change management.
8. Training and Development Manager: Plans, directs, and coordinates programs to enhance employee skills.
9. Human Resources Manager: Oversees recruitment, employee relations, and organizational development.
10. Management Consultant: Advises on business strategies, problem-solving, and organizational improvements.
11. Leadership Development Specialist: Creates programs to develop leadership capabilities within organizations.
12. Performance Coach: Helps individuals improve performance and achieve professional objectives.
13. Business Coach: Guides entrepreneurs in business growth, strategy, and problem-solving.
14. Conflict Resolution Specialist: Aids in resolving disputes and improving communication in workplaces.
15. Executive Search Consultant: Assists organizations in identifying and recruiting executive leadership talent.
16. Team Building Specialist: Designs and facilitates activities to enhance team cohesion.
17. Corporate Trainer: Provides training to improve employee skills and knowledge.
18. Sales Trainer: Develops and delivers training programs to improve sales team performance and effectiveness.
19. Communication Coach: Improves interpersonal communication skills within professional settings.
20. Industrial-Organizational Psychologist: Applies psychological principles to improve workplace dynamics.
21. Change Management Consultant: Guides organizations through change with strategies to ensure smooth transitions.
22. Culture Development Consultant: Aids in cultivating a positive, productive organizational culture.
23. Educational Consultant: Advises on educational strategies, curriculum development, and leadership.
24. Talent Development Specialist: Identifies and nurtures employee talents for organizational growth.
25. Learning and Development Specialist: Designs and implements training programs to promote employee growth and organizational success.

26. Supply Chain Manager: Oversees the end-to-end supply chain process to ensure efficiency and effectiveness.
27. Risk Management Consultant: Helps organizations identify, assess, and mitigate risks.
28. Negotiation Consultant: Aids in enhancing negotiation skills and strategies.
29. Mediator: Facilitates resolution of disputes in a neutral manner.
30. Customer Service Trainer: Improves customer interaction skills of service teams.
31. Process Improvement Consultant: Aids in enhancing operational processes for greater efficiency and productivity.
32. Employee Engagement Consultant: Boosts employee satisfaction and productivity through engagement strategies.
33. Entrepreneurship Advisor: Guides individuals in launching and growing their own businesses.

Appendix No 5

Specializations for Mentors, Coaches and Leaders

1. This compilation presents specialized roles integral to fostering excellence, innovation, and resilience within professional landscapes, offering tailored guidance and support to propel individuals and businesses toward their aspirations.
2. Leadership: Enhancing skills for leading teams and organizations effectively.
3. Performance: Boosting individual or team productivity and output.
4. Career: Navigating career progression and transitions.
5. Sales: Increasing sales proficiency and results.
6. Marketing: Crafting and executing marketing strategies.
7. Strategy: Formulating and applying long-term business plans.
8. Innovation: Fostering creative thinking and new ideas.
9. Culture: Shaping positive organizational values and practices.
10. Conflict Resolution: Managing and resolving disputes effectively.
11. Communication Skills: Improving sharing and receiving of information.
12. Emotional Intelligence: Understanding and managing emotions for improved interactions.
13. Team Dynamics: Strengthening team cooperation and function.
14. Change Leadership: Guiding successful organizational change.
15. Diversity and Inclusion: Building respectful, diverse work environments.
16. Work-Life Balance: Balancing professional responsibilities with personal life.
17. Organizational Development: Enhancing organizational structures and efficiency.
18. Time Management: Prioritizing tasks and managing time wisely.
19. Customer Success: Ensuring clients achieve their desired outcomes.
20. Negotiation Skills: Reaching agreements effectively and advantageously.
21. Personal Branding: Crafting and communicating a personal image.
22. Corporate Governance: Directing company management and policies.
23. Business Ethics: Promoting ethical professional conduct.
24. Financial Coaching for Executives: Managing company finances and economic strategy.
25. Talent Development: Growing employee skills and career paths.
26. Digital Transformation: Integrating digital technology into all business areas.
27. Entrepreneurship: Starting and growing new business ventures.
28. Global Leadership: Leading across diverse cultures and markets.
29. Sustainability Leadership: Integrating eco-friendly practices into business.
30. Crisis Leadership: Leading effectively through emergencies.
31. Mindfulness and Well-being: Promoting mental health and mindfulness practices.

Appendix No 6

Tones

Tone reflects the emotional stance towards the subject or audience, impacting engagement and receptivity. In coaching or leadership, the right tone fosters trust, motivation, and effective communication, aligning with growth-oriented goals.

1. Motivational: Inspiring action and positivity towards achieving goals.
2. Empathetic: Demonstrating understanding and compassion towards others' experiences.
3. Authoritative: Exuding confidence and expertise in guiding others.
4. Inspirational: Provoking thought and encouraging higher aspirations.
5. Supportive: Offering encouragement and backing during challenges.
6. Reflective: Encouraging contemplation and self-assessment.
7. Directive: Providing clear, actionable guidance.
8. Analytical: Examining situations critically and logically.
9. Advisory: Offering suggestions based on expertise.
10. Challenging: Encouraging stretching beyond comfort zones.
11. Respectful: Honoring individuals' values, thoughts, and feelings.
12. Humorous: Adding levity to engage and ease tension.
13. Socratic: Encouraging critical thinking through questioning.
14. Constructive: Providing feedback for growth and improvement.
15. Patient: Showing understanding and tolerance during learning processes.
16. Optimistic: Highlighting the positive and potential success.
17. Realistic: Providing a practical and sensible perspective.
18. Encouraging: Boosting morale and self-efficacy.
19. Appreciative: Acknowledging efforts and achievements.
20. Reassuring: Alleviating concerns and instilling confidence.
21. Inquisitive: Encouraging exploration and curiosity.
22. Observational: Noting and reflecting on behaviors and outcomes.
23. Persuasive: Convincing others towards a certain viewpoint.
24. Resilient: Demonstrating toughness and adaptability in adversity.
25. Visionary: Focusing on long-term potential and broader horizons.
26. Collegial: Promoting a sense of partnership and teamwork.
27. Energizing: Infusing enthusiasm and vigor.
28. Compassionate: Showing care and understanding in dealing with others.
29. Professional: Maintaining a formal and respectful demeanor.
30. Mindful: Demonstrating awareness and consideration.

Appendix No 7

Writing Styles

Writing style denotes how ideas are expressed, encompassing word choice and narrative flow. In coaching, mentoring, and leadership, an apt style clarifies concepts, provides guidance, and facilitates meaningful exploration of ideas.

1. Expository: Explaining facts and information clearly and straightforwardly.
2. Descriptive: Painting a vivid picture to convey a particular scenario or idea.
3. Narrative: Telling a story or recounting events to convey lessons or insights.
4. Persuasive: Arguing a point or encouraging a particular action or mindset.
5. Concise: Delivering information in a brief, direct manner.
6. Analytical: Dissecting information to understand and convey underlying principles.
7. Reflective: Encouraging introspection and consideration of past experiences.
8. Dialogic: Engaging in a two-way conversation to explore ideas.
9. Illustrative: Using examples and anecdotes to clarify points.
10. Instructive: Providing detailed guidance or instructions.
11. Interpretive: Explaining and making sense of complex concepts.
12. Comparative: Analyzing similarities and differences between concepts.
13. Argumentative: Making a case for a particular stance or action.
14. Problem-Solution: Identifying issues and proposing solutions.
15. Evaluative: Assessing the value or effectiveness of certain practices.
16. Journalistic: Reporting facts in an objective, straightforward manner.
17. Exploratory: Delving into topics to discover new insights or perspectives.
18. Contemplative: Encouraging deep thought on certain topics.
19. Case Study: Delving into real-world examples to extract lessons.
20. Research-based: Grounding discourse in empirical evidence.
21. Informal: Adopting a casual, accessible approach.
22. Formal: Adhering to professional language and structure.
23. Technical: Utilizing specialized terminology relevant to the field.
24. Conceptual: Exploring ideas at a high level.
25. Practical: Focusing on actionable advice and real-world application.
26. Empirical: Relying on observation and experience.
27. Theoretical: Delving into theories and abstract concepts.
28. Storyboard: Unfolding ideas through a sequenced narrative.
29. Interactive: Encouraging active engagement from the reader.
30. Scenario-based: Outlining hypothetical situations to explore concepts.

Appendix No 8

Tags

	Chapter	Tag 1	Tag 2	Tag 3
Prompt 1	Accountability	Accountability	Manager Review	Professionalism
Prompt 2	Accountability	Effort Acknowledgment	Team Commitment	Appreciative Strategy
Prompt 3	Accountability	Business Planning	Detailed Explanation	Organizational Structure
Prompt 4	Accountability	Team Dynamics	Goal Accomplishment	Behavioral Mitigation
Prompt 5	Accountability	Motivational Strategies	Perspective Expansion	Opportunity Pursuit
Prompt 6	Awareness	Professional Growth	Development Evaluation	HR Strategies
Prompt 7	Awareness	Self-Awareness	Performance	Management
Prompt 8	Awareness	Identity Recognition	True Self	Personal Growth
Prompt 9	Awareness	Empowerment	Strategy	Contribution
Prompt 10	Awareness	Learning	Access	Productivity
Prompt 11	Awareness	Assumptions	Strategies	Dynamics
Prompt 12	Belief	Empowerment	Beliefs	Goals
Prompt 13	Belief	Mindset	Performance	Belief
Prompt 14	Belief	Outcomes	Emotions	Evaluation
Prompt 15	Belief	Limitations	Independence	Progress
Prompt 16	Belief	Qualities	Development	Professionalism
Prompt 17	Challenge	Independence	Strategies	Motivation
Prompt 18	Challenge	Competencies	Emotional	Resolution
Prompt 19	Challenge	Adaptability	Mindset	Leadership
Prompt 20	Challenge	Systematic	Organization	Guidance
Prompt 21	Challenge	Empowerment	Self-Discovery	Strategies
Prompt 22	Challenge	Risk-Taking	Team-Discussion	Positive-Outcome
Prompt 23	Change	Sales-Communication	Obstacle-Resolution	Client-Service
Prompt 24	Change	Self-Motivation	Performance	Change
Prompt 25	Change	Transformation	Mindset	Improvement
Prompt 26	Commitment	Distribution	Evaluation	Task-Management
Prompt 27	Commitment	Accountability	Performance	Reliability
Prompt 28	Creativity	Creativity	Empowerment	Individuality
Prompt 29	Creativity	Trust	Satisfaction	Loyalty
Prompt 30	Decisions	Evaluation	Strategy	Decision-Making
Prompt 31	Decisions	Decision-Making	Balance	Open-Mindedness
Prompt 32	Excitement	Enthusiasm	Project-Management	Sustainment
Prompt 33	Excitement	Motivation	Energy	Analysis
Prompt 34	Excitement	Motivation	Leadership	Environment
Prompt 35	Fear	Goal-Setting	Fear	Strategy
Prompt 36	Feelings	Emotion-Management	Atmosphere	Leadership
Prompt 37	Feelings	Commitment	Productivity	Assessment
Prompt 38	Feelings	Assessment	Growth	Satisfaction
Prompt 39	Flow	Flow	Engagement	Environment
Prompt 40	Flow	Functioning	Optimization	Workplace
Prompt 41	Fulfillment	Fulfillment	Challenges	Professional-Life
Prompt 42	Fulfillment	Alignment	Passions	Fulfillment

Prompt 43	Goals	Empowerment	Recognition	Problem-Solving
Prompt 44	Goals	Feasibility	Evaluation	Decision-making
Prompt 45	Goals	Fulfillment	Conversations	Emotional
Prompt 46	Habits	Behavior	Analysis	Team-Dynamics
Prompt 47	Habits	Creativity	Perspective	Innovation
Prompt 48	Habits	Networking	Efficacy	Optimism
Prompt 49	Learning	Self-Critique	EmotionalIntelligence	Plan
Prompt 50	Learning	Communication	Engagement	Curiosity
Prompt 51	Learning	Development	Environment	Learning
Prompt 52	Learning	Diplomacy	Self-Awareness	Improvement
Prompt 53	Learning	PersonalGrowth	Effectiveness	Construction
Prompt 54	Learning	Challenge	Motivation	Goals
Prompt 55	Learning	Learning	Engagement	Team-building
Prompt 56	Listening	Communication	Obstacle-Identification	Team-Dynamics
Prompt 57	Mindset	Emotional-Intelligence	Relationship	Assessment
Prompt 58	Mindset	Cognitive	Decision-Making	Fintech
Prompt 59	Mindset	Curiosity	Innovation	Exploration
Prompt 60	Mindset	Empowerment	Responsibility	Decision-Making
Prompt 61	Mindset	Leadership	Self-Management	Emotional-Intelligence
Prompt 62	Options	Resilience	Challenge-Management	Personal-Growth
Prompt 63	Options	Innovation	Problem-Solving	Resilience
Prompt 64	Options	Reflecting	Effectiveness	Decision-making
Prompt 65	Performance	Underperformance	Methodologies	Advertising
Prompt 66	Performance	Evaluation	Performance-Management	Productivity
Prompt 67	Performance	Leadership	Strategies	Step-by-Step
Prompt 68	Preferences	Success	Resilience	Discussion
Prompt 69	Priorities	Self-Management	Autonomy	Independence
Prompt 70	Progress	Communication	Success	Motivation
Prompt 71	Progress	Self-Assessment	Transformation	Leadership
Prompt 72	Progress	Development	Strategies	Engagement
Prompt 73	Purpose	Purpose	Conversation	Hospitality
Prompt 74	Purpose	Communication	Resilience	Remediation
Prompt 75	Purpose	Contribution	Synergy	Alignment
Prompt 76	Relationships	Impact	Morale	Emotional
Prompt 77	Relationships	Satisfaction	Implementation	Interaction
Prompt 78	Relationships	Authenticity	Presence	Interactions
Prompt 79	Relationships	Triggers	Interactions	Compassionate
Prompt 80	Relationships	Engagement	Strategy	Implementation
Prompt 81	Relationships	Dialogue	Professional	Unconventional
Prompt 82	Relationships	Resilience	Fulfillment	Problem-Solving
Prompt 83	Relationships	Habits	Cohesion	Frameworks
Prompt 84	Relationships	Resilience	Introspection	Decision-making
Prompt 85	Relationships	Optimization	Assessment	Efficiency
Prompt 86	Self-assessment	Conflict	Communication	Legal
Prompt 87	Self-assessment	Talent	Assessment	Cohesion
Prompt 88	Self-assessment	Self-awareness	Mindfulness	Growth
Prompt 89	Skills	Skills	Gap	Analysis
Prompt 90	Skills	Skill	Leverage	Metrics

Prompt 91	Strategies	Strategies	KPIs	Alignment
Prompt 92	Strategies	Innovation	Realities	Resource
Prompt 93	Strength	Evolution	Passion	Self-assessment
Prompt 94	Strength	Engagement	Strengths	Metrics
Prompt 95	Strength	Evaluation	Strengths	Allocation
Prompt 96	Strength	Understanding	Strengths	Engagement
Prompt 97	Strength	Impacts	Strengths	Cohesion
Prompt 98	Strength	Alignment	Competency	Realignment
Prompt 99	Strength	Holistic	Fulfillment	Integration
Prompt 100	Support	Support Structures	Needs Assessment	Alignment
Prompt 101	Support	Project Completion	Systems	Stakeholder Buy-in
Prompt 102	Support	Autonomy	Resources	Self-assessment
Prompt 103	Values	Alignment	Engagement	Communication
Prompt 104	Values	Reflection	Identification	Adaptation
Prompt 105	Values	Workshops	Dialogue	Methodologies
Prompt 106	Values	BestPractices	Values	TeamCohesion
Prompt 107	Values	Relationships	Cohesion	Productivity
Prompt 108	Weakness	Strengths	Optimization	Productivity
Prompt 109	Weakness	Team-Weaknesses	Negative-Outcomes	Strategies
Prompt 110	Weakness	Reflection	Artificial-Intelligence	Weaknesses
Prompt 111	Weakness	Improvement	HR	Competencies

Appendix No 9

Unlock the Full Potential of This Book - Instantly

Dive into a world of convenience with our electronic copy!

Feel free to seamlessly copy and paste any prompt that sparks your interest. Customize them to fit your unique needs. Say goodbye to the hassle of retyping. Start crafting your perfect prompts with ease and efficiency!.

To access the electronic copy, please scan this QR code:

www.ingramcontent.com/pod-product-compliance
Lightning Source LLC
LaVergne TN
LVHW082036050326
832904LV00005B/201